Charles Berlitz was born in New York City. He is a graduate of Yale University and a grandson of Maximilian Berlitz, founder of the Berlitz Language Schools. He speaks twenty-five languages with varying degrees of fluency and is considered one of the fifteen most eminent linguists in the world. His interest in archaeology and underwater exploration led to his writing *The Bermuda Triangle* and *The Mystery of Atlantis*. Mr Berlitz was awarded the Dag Hammarskjöld International Prize for Non-fiction. He lives in Florida.

D1494391

By the same author

CHARLES BERLITZ

The Dragon's Triangle

Grafton Books

A Division of HarperCollinsPublishers

GraftonBooks
A Division of HarperCollins*Publishers*
77–85 Fulham Palace Road,
Hammersmith, London W6 8JB

Published in paperback by Grafton Books 1991
9 8 7 6 5 4 3 2 1

First published in Great Britain by
Grafton Books 1990

A CIP catalogue record for this book
is available from the British Library

ISBN 0-586-20778-3

Printed and bound in Great Britain by
Collins, Glasgow

Set in Times

Dedicated to the solution of
the mysteries of the ocean and skies
in an area off the coast of Japan
called the Devil's Sea
or the Dragon Triangle.

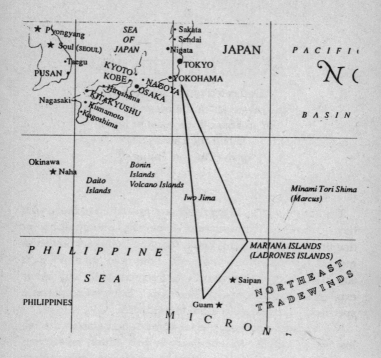

★ Pyongyang

★ Soul (SEOUL)

• Taegu

PUSAN

SEA
OF
JAPAN

• Sakata

• Sendai

• Nigata

JAPAN

PACIFIC

N O

★ TOKYO

KYOTO
KOBE

NAGOYA

YOKOHAMA

Nagasaki

• Hiroshima

KIUKYUSHU

OSAKA

• Kumamoto

• Kagoshima

B A S I N

Okinawa

★ Naha

Daito
Islands

Bonin
Islands

Volcano Islands

Iwo Jima

Minami Tori Shima
(Marcus)

P H I L I P P I N E

S E A

PHILIPPINES

MARIANA ISLANDS
(LADRONES ISLANDS)

★ Saipan

Guam ★

M I C R O N

N O R T H E A S T

T R A D E W I N D S

Acknowledgments

The author wishes to express his appreciation to those who have contributed information, expertise, photographs, or documents for use in this book. Mention in this acknowledgment of any individuals or organizations does not imply their acceptance or knowledge of, or agreement with, any of the explanations or theories in *The Dragon's Triangle* except those specifically attributed to them individually.

The author expresses special appreciation also to the following individuals: Valerie Seary-Berlitz, editor, researcher, author; Mayumi Ogasawara Simms, researcher, calligrapher, writer; Kenzo Ogasawara, geologist, nuclear physicist; Richard Gwynn, author, marine historian, researcher of losses at sea.

The following persons and organizations who have generously contributed information, pictures, and interviews are listed alphabetically: Lin Berlitz, diver, researcher; Caroline Lewis, researcher (Japanese language); David Fasold, author, explorer, Captain, U.S. Merchant Marine; Jay Egloff, oceanographer, geologist (Naval Oceanographic Research Development Organization); Howard Hull, Captain, U.S. Merchant

Marine, and Special Assistant to the President, Maritime Union; Takao Ikeda, researcher and writer; Jane's Information Group, U.S., U.K.; Japan Space Phenomena Society (J.S.P.S.); J.S.R.A., The Shipbuilding Research Association of Japan; Ramona Kashe, Chief of Research for Charles Berlitz in Washington, D.C.; Shigeru Katu, researcher and writer (J.S.P.S.); Kyodo News Service; Dr. Talbot Lindstrom, former Deputy Under Secretary of Defense, U.S.A.; Lloyds Maritime Information Service, U.K.; Robert Loughman (Jane's); Robert McCann, photographer; R. Misumida, President, Nikkai Marine Co., Ltd., Tokyo; National Maritime Museum, Greenwich, London, U.K.; Ivan T. Sanderson, author, explorer, zoologist, founder of S.I.T.U.; Katie Sears, researcher (Chinese language); Shin-ichiro Namiki, President, J.S.P.S.; The Society for the Investigation of the Unexplained (S.I.T.U.), which offered the use of its files and quarterly publication *Pursuit*; Bob Warth, President, S.I.T.U., research chemist, investigator, world traveler; The World Ship Society, Devon, U.K.; and Dr. J. Manson Valentine, Ph.D., author, explorer, zoologist, investigator of phenomena, scientist, research associate of the Bishop Museum, Honolulu, Curator Honoris of the Museum of Science, Miami, Florida.

And special appreciation to William Thompson, Editor-in-Chief; Catherine Cook, Associate Editor; and Bernard Kurman, literary agent, for their encouragement and understanding.

Much of the first-published information about the Dragon Triangle comes from the press of Japan, the Philippines, Great Britain, the West Coast of the United States, Australia, New Zealand, and Hong Kong, in other words, the countries whose losses were at issue. But if we drew a line encompassing the countries mentioned above, we would indicate the boundaries of the "Ring of Fire" of the Pacific, with special emphasis on the ocean islands and coasts of Japan.

It may be that the gulfs will wash us down.

—Tennyson, "Ulysses"

Heere be dragons.

—from a medieval map of the sea

Contents

THE
DRAGON'S
TRIANGLE

1

Another Triangle of Doom

On the other side of the world from the Bermuda Triangle there exists a section of the ocean startlingly similar in its history of vanishing ships and planes. The Japanese have been aware of this dangerous area for a thousand years. They have called it the Ma–no Umi: the Sea of the Devil. For centuries, seamen have attributed the repeated mysterious losses of fishing boats to sea demons, restless dragons who come to the surface of the ocean to seize fishing boats and drag them and their occupants down to the dragons' underwater lairs.

It is no coincidence that the Bermuda Triangle is sometimes called the Devil's Triangle, for when tragic events cannot be logically explained, it is always easy to put the blame on the devil or other unfriendly supernatural entities.

In the case of the Bermuda Triangle, sudden and unexplained disappearances of surface craft and aircraft have often been attributed to electromagnetic anomalies, mysterious weather conditions, and even exploratory UFOs which either spacenap craft from Earth or cause them, by use of extraterrestrial power sources, to disintegrate and sink beneath the ocean.

Over the last fifteen years, the Bermuda Triangle has achieved an awesome celebrity—or rather, notoriety—all over the world as a place of mystery. Numerous books, not to mention magazine and newspaper articles, have been devoted to the disappearances of sailing vessels and aircraft in the Bermuda Triangle, as well as to the other strange phenomena associated with this section of the Atlantic.

The Bermuda Triangle and the Ma–no Umi—the Dragon Triangle—share many of the more believable but no less dangerous characteristics. The triangles constitute the two areas of the world most known for compass deviations, malfunction and nonfunction of radio communication, huge unexpected waves, seaquakes, minicanes (intense localized hurricanes), great whirlpools, and sudden and localized fogs.

Above all, both areas are known for the disappearance of scores of ships and planes, together with their crews and passengers, leaving no identifiable flotsam to indicate the cause of their vanishing.

Far more important than the lost craft, however, is the matter of the death, if they really died, of thousands of people: naval and merchant seamen, air crews, passengers, and fishermen. And in the Dragon Sea, a number of marine scientists must be added to the roll call of the lost. While probing for the cause of so many mysterious disappearances in the Dragon Triangle, these men of science have also disappeared, along with their research vessels.

A curious coincidence does occur in the Japanese term for

a type of wave encountered in the seas of the Dragon Triangle. It is called *sankaku-nami*, "triangle wave," meaning that these waves appear to head toward a ship from three directions, all at the same time.

Like the Bermuda Triangle, the Dragon Triangle in the Western Pacific forms a generally triangular pattern. It follows a line from western Japan north of Tokyo to a point in the Pacific at approximately latitude 145 degrees east. It then turns west-southwest past the Ogasawara Shinto (the Bonin Islands) and then down to Guam and Yap, west to Taiwan and then returns north-northeast back to Japan, near the measuring point of Nojima Zaki on the Bay of Tokyo. The Bermuda Triangle is generally considered to go approximately from the Straits of Florida north-northeast to Bermuda, south to the Lesser Antilles and back to Florida.

These two triangles share strange characteristics when plotted on a globe. They appear on exactly opposite sides of the earth. They are both located on longitude 35 degrees west and east respectively. And, if we take the western edge of the Bermuda Triangle at latitude 50 degrees north and follow it over the top of the world, we find that it descends through the Dragon Triangle. In other words, the two triangles are on opposite sides of the earth's crust for both latitude *and* longitude. But the similarities do not end here.

The two areas are both located at the eastern end of continental masses, the drop-off to deep water where the sea is swept by strong currents over active volcanic areas. The sea floor varies from relatively shallow areas to the plunging depths of the ocean's deepest trenches.

In the Bermuda Triangle the trench north of Puerto Rico extending west into the Caribbean is as deep as any area of the Atlantic.

In the case of the Dragon Triangle, the entire eastern coast of Japan is close to great gulfs in the ocean floor—the Ogasawara Deep, and the Ryukyu, Mariana, and Philippine trenches. In 1960, the U.S. bathyscape *Trieste* touched bottom at 36,198 feet in the Mariana Trench. If Mount Everest, 29,028 feet high, were to rise from this abyss, it would still be over a mile below the surface of the waves.

There exists a possibility, in both cases, of finding unknown creatures and unsuspected forces in the depths of these oceanic black holes.

Another element common to the two triangles concerns the agonic lines (from the Greek, meaning "no angles"). While these lines are invisible, they reflect a measurable peculiarity of the earth's magnetic field. The north and south magnetic poles do not coincide with the geographic north and south poles. Thus, the connecting force lines between the magnetic poles north and south do not line up exactly with the meridians of longitude. The paths to these two sets of poles do not coincide except for the general north-south direction.

The meridians appear on all maps, and are exact and numbered as to degrees; but the agonic lines follow paths that are modified and sometimes wandering. At certain places on the earth, they coincide with the meridians, and only then does the compass needle point true north, instead of the customary isogonic reading, up to an angle of 20 degrees with the meridian. This coincidence may result in occasional misreading of compasses—with adverse results.

The principle agonic line in the Western Hemisphere runs through the Bermuda Triangle, while the main agonic line in the Eastern Hemisphere runs through the Dragon Triangle.

In both triangles, magnetism, perhaps intensified, has often affected compasses and caused ships and planes to lose direction. Perhaps, since knowledge about the earth's interior is still largely theoretical, a great electromagnetic field may lie between these two diametrically opposed triangles, working through the huge cosmic dynamo that is our home planet.

In his book *The Encyclopedia of the Unknown*, Colin Wilson offers a magnetically related solution to the disappearance problem. Although birds have used the magnetic lines to navigate on their migrations since time immemorial, observers have noticed situations in which flocks have inexplicably lost their way, perhaps due to an anomaly in the planet's magnetic field.

The *Marine Observer* for 1930 cautioned seamen about a magnetic disturbance at the Tambora volcano, near the island of Sumbawa in Indonesia, a disturbance which could deflect a ship's compass by as much as 6 degrees. Captain Stutt of the ship *Australia* encountered a similar anomaly—one powerful enough to deflect his ship's compass by 12 degrees!

Wilson also connects fluctuations in the earth's magnetic field with the rubbing and pressure of the great tectonic plates which make up our planet's crust. He goes on to say:

Scientists are not sure why the earth has a magnetic field, but one theory suggests that it is due to movement in its molten core. Such movements would in fact produce shifting patterns in the earth's field, and bursts of magnetic activity, which might be compared to the burst of solar energy known as sunspots. If they *are* related to earth-tensions and therefore to earthquakes, then we would expect them to occur in certain definite zones just as earthquakes do. What effects would a sudden "earthquake" of magnetic activity produce? One would be to cause compasses to spin, for it would be rather as if a huge magnetic meteor was roaring up from the center of the earth. On the seas it would produce an effect of violent turbulence, for it would affect the water in the same way the moon affects the tides, but in an irregular pattern, so that the water would appear to be coming "from all directions."

The description of the water effects of such an anomaly sounds very similar to that of the *sankaku-nami*—the dreaded triangle wave encountered in the Dragon Triangle. Perhaps those who survived to report this frightening phenomenon actually lived through only a weak demonstration of the force of magnetic anomalies. And, given the tectonic origins of such anomalies, it should be noted that the Dragon Sea and environs are among the most tectonically active areas in the world.

The Bermuda Triangle has attracted public attention since December 5, 1945, when the collective disappearance of five Aztec Avenger torpedo bombers took place between the east coast of Florida and the Bahamas, followed by the disappearance of a Martin Mariner search plane. The search for this "Lost Patrol" involved hundreds of planes and surface craft, yet no wreckage or any clues to the fate of men and planes were ever discovered. The radio messages from the "Lost Patrol" implied that they were flying over islands that were not on their charts or "not where they were supposed to be." In the light of subsequent developments in the Bermuda Triangle, it has been suggested that the planes might have somehow crossed back in time, when there were more and different islands off the coast of Florida.

The case is still open in naval archives, and public interest in the fate of the Aztec Avengers still flares up every time the remains of a plane of this type are found on the sea bottom or in the Florida Everglades. On each occasion an unsuccessful attempt has been made to compare the engine numbers of the discovered plane with those of the Lost Patrol's planes. What happened to them and where they went, along with hundreds of other large and small planes and ships since that time, remains a mystery.

The strange and mysterious incidents within the Dragon Triangle have been well known in Japan and other nearby islands for a much longer time than the occurrences in the Bermuda Triangle. Ships have been recorded as disappearing in the Dragon Triangle for more than a thousand years (some researchers say 3,000 years). Ancient records show that this mysterious sea has claimed ships from the days of the Sung and Yuan dynasties of China and the medieval Japanese shogunates until the present day.

Chinese legends dating back to 900 B.C. tell of a dragon's underwater "palace" located beneath a small island five or six days' sail from Suzhou, in Kiangsu province. Even on windless days the seas in the locality were too rough for ships to approach safely. Strange noises could be heard by those venturing close—and strange lights visible for a hundred miles shone over the water by night.

Now, nearly three millennia later, ships over 200,000 tons, carrying oil, coal, and other bulk cargo, have vanished in this area, leaving no crew members, identifiable wreckage, or flotsam to indicate what happened. Perhaps there is something more here at work than ancient sailors' tales.

Naval and scientific interest was first aroused in Japan when it was noted that a number of patrol ships and commercial fishing craft of fairly light tonnage, up to 190 tons, had vanished within a few years of 1945 off the east coast of Japan. The toll of missing personnel, augmented by the presumed drownings of crews from larger ships that regularly disappeared, impelled the Japanese Shipping Administration as early as 1950 to proclaim the Iza and Ogasawara island chains as an official danger area for ships.

Regarding the Bermuda Triangle, the Seventh Coast Guard District, responsible for rescues in the area, has received thousands of letters from small-craft owners, asking whether the Bermuda Triangle is really a dangerous area. The answer from Seventh USCG District comes as a form letter:

Mysterious, mystic, supernatural . . . unlikely! This area, commonly bounded by Bermuda, Florida, and Puerto Rico, might have on the surface what would be considered a high disappearance rate, but you also have to consider the amount of air and sea traffic in this area. Thousands of ships, small boats, and commercial and private aircraft transit the waters off Florida's east coast. The majority of disappearances in this area can be attributed to its unique environmental features. . . .

There are some possible justifications and so-called mysterious disappearances within the area, but the coast guard is not impressed with explanations from the supernatural. . . .

In other words, while the coast guard steadfastly denies the existence of such an area as the Bermuda Triangle, it provides the coordinates (apparently so that boaters will know when they are in the triangle, in case it really does exist). This official opinion, however, is not shared by coastguardsmen who continue to have unusual and startling experiences within its boundaries.

It is notable, however, that the coast guard's letter mentions another "trouble spot" in the world:

An area called the "Devil's Sea" by Japanese and Filipino seamen, located off the east coast of Japan, also exhibits the same magnetic characteristics. Like the "Bermuda Triangle," it is known for its mysterious disappearances.

That these disappearances continue right on the well-trafficked doorsteps of two of the developed world's leaders in electronics, computers, and high technology must be considered mysterious indeed.

It is interesting to note that the two principal danger areas are located to the east of continent-sized land masses, in locations where warm and cold ocean currents collide. The warm currents generally head north, while the cold currents head south. These are also nodal points marking the turns of both surface ocean currents and the tidal currents deep below the ocean's surface. Again, these currents usually turn in opposite directions.

The strength of these great flowing masses of water may generate a more powerful pull than that of the north magnetic pole, creating magnetic anomalies in space and time.

Certainly, as Ivan Sanderson has pointed out, there are some interesting time effects to be found in these areas: cases of carefully clocked airline flights arriving early, sometimes so far ahead of their ETA (estimated time of arrival) that the only explanation would be 500 mile per hour tail winds!

The passengers of such flights should feel congratulated not only for an unexpectedly early arrival, but for safe passage through a space-time anomaly that has sent so many other travelers on a one-way passage to oblivion.

The heavily traveled shipping lanes of the Bermuda Triangle were the happy hunting grounds of many German submarines during World War II, which surely must account for many ship vanishings. The Dragon Triangle, besides submarine activity, saw some of the most serious surface fighting of the war.

Nonmysterious disappearances of Japanese vessels include the sinking of the aircraft carriers *Taiho* and *Shokaku* along with 340 planes in the Battle of the Philippine Sea; the loss of the carrier *Zuikako* with four battleships, three other aircraft carriers, ten heavy cruisers, and nine destroyers in the Japanese escape from Leyte Gulf; and the loss of five ships and 4,000 kamikaze planes at Okinawa. One of the vessels was the huge battleship *Yamato*, sent into battle with insufficient fuel for a return voyage. Considering such known losses, any disappearances during World War II have not been considered as mysteries in either triangle, given the proliferation of mines, submarines, and air strikes during that time.

An exception should be made, however, for the simultaneous mass disappearance of five Japanese warships at the beginning of 1942 while on maneuvers close to the shores of Japan. The flotilla comprised three destroyers and two small aircraft carriers. What happened to these ships was never ascertained. It is extremely doubtful that they were sunk by enemy action, since they were in home waters and neither the United States nor Great Britain had, during those dark early days of the war, ships or submarines in the area. Colonel Jimmy Doolittle's bombing raid on Tokyo was months away, as was the Battle of Midway, where the Japanese fleet sustained its first heavy losses. In any case, the Allies would assuredly have quickly taken credit for any sinkings if their forces had been involved.

The history of the early naval war in the Pacific yields another interesting footnote. United States submarine forces were greatly hampered in their operations off the shores of Japan because the magnetic detonators on their torpedos worked incorrectly. At times, torpedos would actually turn to attack the ships that had launched them. Although the magnetic detonators represented the best technology of the time, the navy's torpedo arsenal had to be refitted with contact detonators.

Reminiscent of similar incidents in the Bermuda Triangle is another recorded wartime incident in the Dragon Triangle, apparently not connected with combat. This occurred toward the end of the Pacific War. In *The Deadly Mystery of Japan's Bermuda Triangle*, Rufus Drake quotes Shiro Kawamoto, commander of a Zero fighter wing, who stated that a last radio message had been received from the pilot of a Kawanishi Flying Boat prior to the invasion of Iwo Jima. The plane was on patrol during a night when no United States aircraft had been reported in the area. The last message from the Kawanishi was a curious one. The pilot said, "Something is happening in the sky . . . the sky is opening up—." There was no further communication—the plane vanished.

We have no way of knowing if something similar happened to military U.S. and Japanese planes that have vanished in this area within recent years, for whatever happened to them happened too quickly for the pilots to send a message.

After the end of World War II and the reopening of Japan's sea lanes, ship disappearances and mysterious sinkings continued to occur in the Dragon Triangle. From 1949 to 1954 ten large fishing vessels and coast guard cutters vanished without a trace and with all witnesses—totaling hundreds of people—lost.

One such ship, the *Kaiō Maru No. 5*, vanished in 1952 while on a research expedition to find out why the area was so dangerous. Its disappearance was notable because the sea was calm at the time and the weather was excellent. Although the vessel had 150 tons of oil on board, no oil slick was found on the surface near its last check-in message. Nothing unusual was said over the radio, which functioned up to the time of the disappearance.

The only flotsam found were five undamaged empty oil barrels. Explanations concerning the loss of the *Kaiō Maru No. 5* include the theories that it had been sunk by a Russian submarine, sideswiped by a large United States naval craft, or had even been blown out of the water by an undersea volcano. A Japanese magazine, quoting accounts of ancient legends still believed in the area, suggested that dragons or giant squid had swallowed the ship at one gulp.

Mysterious losses of ships and planes have continued through the years, and these include cargo ships, tankers, ore ships, and fishing vessels, as well as passenger and military aircraft. March 1957, the so-called nightmare month in the history of aviation, included three air disappearances within a two-week period in the Dragon Triangle. Unexplained losses of ships and planes have continued up to the present.

While we of course have no interviews with personnel from ships that have vanished, a certain number of vessels have touched the fringes of oblivion. Yet even here, frustratingly, the survivors often can give no coherent account of what befell them or their ships. As the following chapter shows, modern technology, communications, and professional experience are still insufficient to ward off or even explain the dangers of the Dragon Triangle.

2

A Roll Call of Disappearances

Disappearances of ships over or near the great trenches of the Pacific, west of Japan and extending down the China Sea, have been occurring for well over a thousand years. In former times, when any legend was generally credible, many believed the ships had sunk as the result of dragons stirring up the sea, devils causing engulfing whirlpools, and even, in a legend once current in the Japanese oceanic islands, unexpected tidal waves caused by a change of position of a cosmically giant shrimp on the abyssal ocean bottom.

Even a modern navigator, with the best of technology at his command, would take pause at the number of natural hazards in the area—typhoons with winds of over 200 miles per hour, volcanic and tectonic activity, with actual volcanic eruptions, earthquakes and tsunamis, seiche waves caused by enormous undersea landslides in the vast oceanic trenches, and unknown activity in the ocean currents. In 1963, oceanographers didn't even suspect the existence of the Cromwell Current, running deep under the sea. A few years later, this current inexplicably rose to the surface of the Pacific, then sank once again.

It was only after World War II, with the increase of marine traffic necessary for the rebuilding of Japan's cities and economy, that a series of total disappearances and sinkings of ships began to be noted. Quickly, it became evident that the reputation of the Ma–no Umi was even more menacing than previously thought. This area, even in comparison with the Bermuda Triangle, seemed to constitute the most dangerous section of the world's seas and oceans.

Beginning in the early 1970s, public attention, in Japan at least, began to focus on the growing number of disappearances and sinkings, first on light-tonnage ships and aircraft, then on larger vessels, and finally on the enormous tankers so necessary for the importing of oil into Japan and for Japan's export industry.

Although reports of shipping losses in the Dragon Triangle have been carried on the major wire services, especially Reuters, the language barrier has indubitably hampered worldwide appreciation of the situation in the Dragon Triangle. Stories that appear in major Japanese newspapers like *Asahi Shimbun* do not always find their way into their counterparts in the English-speaking world. Certainly, the immediate postwar losses in the Triangle were treated as a minor, localized phenomenon, even when reported in the world press.

One wonders how general the knowledge of the Bermuda Triangle might be today, if so much of the area (and the ships, crews, and owners) hadn't been connected to English-speaking nations.

However, from all accounts, both English and Japanese, the ships and planes lost in the Dragon Triangle have left no trace. They have all apparently descended into the depths of the Western Pacific trenches, from which their retrieval would be physically or economically impossible.

Other sunken ships such as the *Andrea Doria*, portions of the Imperial Japanese Fleet at Truk, and the United States warships at Pearl Harbor were relatively easy to find and research, since they were near harbors at the time they went down. And the mast of the German heavy cruiser *Graf Spee* still protrudes from the Atlantic's surface to mark the ship's position on the shallow sea bottom near Montevideo.

Other German and British ships sunk in the war have also been located, as have the majority of torpedoed passenger liners. In the Mediterranean, the Baltic, the English Channel, and the waters off Florida, salvage operations have been attempted on ships as diverse as ancient Greek merchantmen and Roman galleys, a lost flagship of the seventeenth-century Swedish fleet, King Henry VIII's flagship, and numerous Spanish galleons. As most of these had been discovered in relatively shallow water, or their position had been known, their locations were explored by those in search of treasure, either in the form of gold, prize cargo, publicity, or archaeological and maritime information.

Even the lost *Titanic* has been located deep on the ocean floor of the North Atlantic, and probed by unmanned submersibles operating by remote control. The grand ballroom that had been unseen for more than seventy years has now been revisited, and televised all over the world.

But the search for lost and derelict ships is not always easy. Besides its great depth, the Pacific is also the world's largest ocean, stretching more than 10,000 miles. Its storms are more violent, simply because they have more space to develop before hitting land. And winds and currents can sometimes take a derelict or traces of a wreck to unexpected places. One case in point involves the Pacific's most celebrated ghost ship, the *Joyita*, which was found drifting nearly 500 miles away from its expected location.

Even more impressive is the strange journey of the *Dalgonar*, a British vessel which was caught in a storm in the middle South Pacific in 1913. After the ship had lost its masts and capsized, the crew was heroically rescued by another sailing ship, the *Loire*. The abandoned ship was left to sink. Instead, more than two years later, the hulk of the *Dalgonar* stranded on a reef in the Society Islands—a good two thousand miles from the area where it was supposed to have sunk.

Floating derelicts have always been a concern in the maritime world, since they may threaten to sink other ships in the sea lanes. This is especially true when the hulks of dead ships are slightly below the water's surface and thus invisible to the crew on watch. As late as 1894, shipping sources had traced 1,628 derelict ships floating in the North Atlantic alone. The courses of these moving ships helped oceanographers trace the course of the Gulf Stream.

And it is not so long ago that the coast guard had the unenviable task of tracking and sinking derelicts to the number of 200 a year. It is grimly ironic that one of the capsized wrecks actually had survivors trapped in its hull—a real-life precursor to the book and movie *The Poseidon Adventure*. Luckily, this particular derelict was found and the crewmen rescued before the coast guard had a chance to do its duty and sink the wreck.

However, the toll of ships and aircraft missing in the Dragon Triangle since the end of World War II surely makes one of the strangest stories of the Pacific. The most striking aspect is that all were lost without any message indicating what was happening, almost as if whatever caused them to disappear occurred too quickly to report over the radio—or was not noticed until too late to report.

The mystery only deepens, both literally and figuratively, since the only logical resting place for the lost ships is the ocean trenches. Even if wreckage were to escape from these incredible depths, the intense water pressure may have altered it beyond recognition. This same awesome pressure effectively prohibits any investigation of deep-lying wreckage. It is most difficult for researchers to solve an enigma when any evidence remains in stygian darkness six miles below the sea, under tons of ocean pressure.

The toll of lost ships includes only the larger surface craft that have been made a matter of record. The maritime boards in some countries put limits on what losses should be reported. For instance, the U.S. Board of Investigation specifies that a formal investigation requires:

1. That a ship sinking include the taking of six or more lives
2. That the sinking involve the loss of 100 tons or more

While all the losses detailed on the next pages would amply qualify for such requirements, an unknown number of smaller craft, as recorded by only memory and tradition, have vanished in the Dragon Triangle during the last thousand years. This expanded but still partial listing is the result of cross-checking with Japanese maritime investigation sources and Lloyds of London records for lost ships.

Vessel and Flag	Tonnage	Date Last Message Received	Location	Crew Lost
Kuroshio Maru No. 1 Japan	1,525	19 April 1949	Dragon Triangle	23
Kuroshio Maru No. 2 Japan	1,525	22 April 1949	Dragon Triangle	22
Chōfuku Maru No. 5 Japan	66	8 June 1952	East of Okurajima	29
Kaiō Maru No. 5 (Maritime Safety Agency) Japan	500	24 September 1952	Myojinsho	31
Shinsei Maru Japan	62	6 June 1953	Oga-sawara Shotō	17
Kōchi Maru No. 16 Japan	150	December 1953	East of Iwo Jima	22
Kuroshio Maru No. 3 Japan	1,525	20 January 1954	East of Nishino-shima	18
Fuyō Maru No. 2 Japan	227	25 September 1954	Near Miyake-jima	25
Seisho Maru No. 1 Japan	190	20 October 1954	Southeast of Okura-jima	25
Chiyo Maru No. 15 Japan	18	6 December 1954	Kinansho	12

Vessel and Flag	Tonnage	Date Last Message Received	Location	Crew Lost
USAF *F-3B* Aircraft USA	——	26 June 1955	After take-off from Atsugi AB	Not known
USAF *KB-50* Aircraft USA	——	12 March 1957	Between Wake and Japan	8
USN *JD-1* Invader Aircraft USA	——	16 March 1957	Between Japan and Okinawa	5
USAF *C-97* Aircraft USA	——	22 March 1957	Southeast of Japan	67
Donan Maru Japan	2,849	7 June 1963	Off Shionomisaki	33
Juno Panama	1,385	10 October 1964	South of Japan	21
Denny Rose UK	6,656	13 September 1967	South of Japan	42
Tong Hong UK	4,690	25 October 1967	No message after leaving Kawasaki	38
Agios Giorgis Greece	16,565	8 January 1970	Dragon Triangle	29
JA-341 Aircraft Japan	——	10 February 1970	Flying south of Chōshi	3

Vessel and Flag	Tonnage	Date Last Message Received	Location	Crew Lost
P2V Anti-submarine Patrol Aircraft Japan	——	16 July 1971	55 miles northeast of Tokyo	11
Banaluna Liberia	13,616	12 November 1971	En route to Kokura	35
Junior KL Philippines	2,470	5 October 1971	China Sea	Not Specified
Sea Pine Panama	1,794	6 October 1971	Left Japan for Taiwan	26
Geranium France	232	24 November 1974	En route to Osaka	29
Transocean Shipper Philippines	9,275	16 February 1975	Left Wakayama	33
Ming Song Panama	891	22 October 1975	North of Australia	17
Berge Istra Liberia	227,912	29 December 1975	Between Japan and Philippines	40
Don Aurelio Panama	4,066	9 January 1976	In Japanese waters en route to Philippines	31
New Venture Panama	7,194	30 June 1976	North of Bataan	30

Vessel and Flag	Tonnage	Date Last Message Received	Location	Crew Lost
Rose S Liberia	1,720	13 February 1977	En route to Osaka	31
Triumph No. 1 Panama	8,342	22 February 1977	Off Japan	Not Specified
Hae Dang Wha South Korea	102,805	28 July 1980	Off Japan en route to Korea	29
Derbyshire UK	169,044	September 1980	South of Tokyo Bay	44
Dunav Yugoslavia	14,712	28 December 1980	Southeast of Cape Nojima	31
Antiparos Greece	13,862	2 January 1981	En route to Osaka	35
Glomar Java Sea UK	5,930	October 1983	Off Hainan Island	81
Maasgusar Liberia	Not available	14 March 1987	Dragon Triangle	23
Queen Jane Panama	9,909	23 October 1987	Near Taiwan	24

Reports concerning one missing ship lost with all hands and later located while submerged have the elements of a James Bond scenario. The *Glomar Java Sea*, 5,930 tons, an oil-drilling vessel, was found submerged off Hainan Island in October 1983, with thirty-four bodies out of a crew of eighty-one.

All crewmen were presumed dead, although rumors were received that some had been picked up by Vietnamese fishing boats and sent to prison camps in Vietnam. The large number of crew members and the unconfirmed reports about the captured survivors seem to underline the opinion of Captain David Whitton, a member of the board of investigation, who said, "This is not a normal accident and it has no precedent."

The danger of a heavily laden ship carrying iron and sailing in stormy weather was emphasized in the case of the *Dunav*, which vanished in 1980 before it could stop at Yokahama as planned, just after sending a report that it had incurred a water leak. It did not, however, send an SOS. Search for the *Dunav* started on January 1, but no oil slick, flotsam, or survivors were found.

Some days after the search for the *Dunav* began, another ship, the *Antiparos*, disappeared a short time before it was scheduled to dock at Osaka. The *Antiparos* was carrying 21,410 tons of scrap iron. Both ships vanished on the main shipping lanes from the United States to Japan, and should have been easy to find. The break-off of contact and complete disappearances brought renewed press interest to the area of doom west of Japan.

The *Rose S*, a 514-foot cargo ship carrying scrap iron and logs, was unlike most of the ships which have disappeared in the Dragon Triangle. This vessel managed to send a distress call before it vanished, although not specifying what was wrong. Searchers reaching the area noticed some logs, which could also have come from other log-carrying ships, but no sign of the *Rose S*.

The Maritime Safety Agency ship *Kaiō Maru No. 5*, which disappeared while on its search for clues of other ship disappearances, was finally judged to be the victim of an undersea volcanic explosion. Every section of the Dragon Sea was searched, and all that was found were a few pieces of debris with pumice flakes clinging to them. From this thin evidence, it was decided that the ship had overturned during an underwater volcanic eruption. Even representatives of the Science Agency were not satisfied, complaining of "many matters left unknown."

Besides twenty-two crew members, nine scientists were lost aboard the *Kaiō Maru No. 5*, including geologists and oceanographers. That so many trained observers should be lost to the phenomenon they set out to study simply compounds the mystery with frustration.

The *Kaiō Maru* was not the only research vessel that disappeared in this area. Another, the *Kuroshio Maru No. 3*, also vanished without an SOS while on a research expedition to locate favorable fishing grounds. The loss of these two research ships, apart from the data they may have gathered, was a seemingly irrefutable indication that the Dragon Triangle holds unexpected dangers.

Still further proof comes with the discovery of a Liberian-registered tanker, the *Maasgusar*, drifting derelict in mysterious circumstances. A patrol discovered the vessel engulfed in flames off the coast of Japan. The *Maasgusar* had been carrying a cargo of 27,500 tons of flammable toxic liquids. A huge hole in the ship's chemical tanks pointed to the possibility of an explosion. There was no sign of the twenty-three crew members.

The losses detailed in the above chart do not include sinkings of ships in the Dragon Triangle where there were survivors or other witnesses, such as crews of neighboring ships. Yet even when ships are not lost without a trace, the information available from survivors does very little to dispel the enigma of the Dragon Triangle. Most of these disasters were imperfectly perceived by survivors amid the chaos of sinking.

Among smaller craft, tremendous numbers of commercial fishing boats in the Dragon Triangle have disappeared each year for centuries. These losses have generally been attributed to the vagaries of the sea. Only in fairly recent years has an annual count of losses been calculated. These are the loss figures for several years, as released by the Japanese Maritime Safety Agency:

1968	Boats missing, cause unknown, no trace: 521
1970	Boats missing, cause unknown, no trace: 435
1972	Boats missing, cause unknown, no trace: 471

As there usually had been no message or SOS, there is no explanation as to what happened to these ships or their crews, nor any recognizable wreckage. It must also be noted that the incredibly high loss statistics for small vessels in this area for any one of these years outstrips the total number of all vessels lost in the Bermuda Triangle since 1860.

In ancient and medieval times the crews of small fishing craft found it easy to accept tales of sea monsters which attacked and often demolished their boats. And today too, the disappearances of ships with modern equipment and the most up-to-date means of communication in this area have evoked a certain memory of regional tales and the old legends of these sea monsters, the dragons.

In sum, both mysterious triangles have sustained peacetime losses out of proportion to those of any other body of water in the world. But there exists an intriguing difference. The losses in the Bermuda Triangle have generally occurred to small craft and pleasure boats, many of which were skippered by their owners. In addition to such small craft, the Dragon Triangle has also claimed much larger merchant ships, as well as patrol boats and commercial fishing vessels under the command of experienced captains.

Radio and check-in information from larger craft are more closely followed by the ship-owning companies than is the case with small, owner-operated craft. But the large cargo ships and tankers vanish in the Dragon Triangle just as swiftly and without warning as the smaller craft in the Bermuda

Triangle. There is an unnatural aspect to these disappearances, as if elements other than the weather and sea are involved.

There is no comparison between the two triangles in tonnage or size of ships and cargoes lost. Consider the gigantic ships described in the following chapter. The *Berge Istra*, 227,912 DWT (dead weight tons), was five times larger than the *Titanic*. The *Derbyshire* and the *Hae Dang Wha*, 169,044 and 102,805 DWT respectively.

The circumstances concerning the sinking of these huge ships remain a mystery, and submarine investigation, as we now know it, is not likely to clarify what has happened to these ships if they lie in the bottom of the trenches off Japan—trenches nearly six miles deep.

3

Great Ships That Sailed into Oblivion

The Pacific Ocean is perhaps the most romantic and storied of the great bodies of water. It is home to myriad tropical islands with names that conjure up exotic images of adventure and mystery. Writers such as Robert Louis Stevenson and James Michener, as well as artists like Gauguin, have described the Pacific environment and burned its brilliance into the Western mind. The enduring image of the area is that of untamed island beauty, peaceful lagoons, and transparent ocean waters.

Unfortunately, the real Pacific, with its storms and uneasy seismic balance, often belies the imagery. And one corner of this mighty ocean is an especially volatile and life-threatening locale. This, of course, is the area bounded by the islands of

Japan, the Philippines, and the Marianas—the place known as the Dragon Triangle.

The Dragon Triangle is plagued by many violent, unexpected, and unpredictable storms. There are several possible scientific explanations for this. In the Pacific region, air flowing from the Asian continent is usually cold and dry. Air currents grow strongest as they pass over the continent's east coast and commonly form storms which travel east, directly into the Dragon Triangle.

The formation of sudden, violent storms is aided by the 1- to 3-degree Centigrade deviation in ocean temperature possible in the Triangle. Storms passing over a water mass which is alternately cold and warm become erratic and their behavior impossible to predict. Such weather patterns pose unusual hazards to shipping and air traffic. A similar breeding spot for storms is in the Gulf Stream off the Atlantic coast of North America—the infamous Bermuda Triangle.

The killer hurricane known as the typhoon is justly feared in the Dragon Triangle and China Sea. Big ships caught in a typhoon invariably seek the safety of the open ocean and deep water where they hope to ride out the storm. Small ships unable to make harbor are unlikely to survive.

Two of these typhoons hit Japan in rapid succession in September 1945. The first passed ninety miles east of the islands, but even at that distance, the winds which battered the Japanese home islands exceeded sixty knots. The tiny American minesweepers YMS-98 and YMS-472 raced before the storm toward Okinawa and safe harbor, only to miss the turn at the northern tip of the island. They disappeared into the storm—and only one man survived. The YMS-421 and YMS-341, traveling to Buckner Bay from Saipan and Guam, capsized and sank just outside of the harbor. Luckily, most of their crewmen were rescued.

The next typhoon to devastate Buckner Bay packed winds

gusting to 144 knots. This monster storm sank the ships *Mona Island*, *Southard*, *Dorsey* (whose crew had to hang on to wreckage until noon the next day before they were rescued), the *Weehawken*, *Snowbell*, the YMSs 146, 151, 384, and the AMC-86. A full week after the typhoon, thirty-six ships were still aground in the bay, and 1,400 sailors were still homeless.

Fortunately, today typhoons can be monitored and tracked. However, when trapped by one there is little a ship's crew can do but stay calm and pray. One American skipper of a mine-sweeper, sailing with a group of small boats, found his ship in dire straits during a typhoon. He frantically radioed his commander.

"Burgundy! Burgundy!"

"This is Burgundy. Go ahead," came the response.

"Er—ah—I think my mast is going to break . . . ooops! There it goes now."

Burgundy answered sardonically: "Roger. Out."

The main ocean current in the region, the North Equatorial Current, runs east to west, twisting and turning along its way in a spiral-like fashion. The current branches just east of the Philippines; one branch runs south along the coast of Mindanao while the larger hugs the east coast of the Philippines and the island of Formosa. It continues northeast, diving between the ridges supporting the Ryukyu Islands, then twists east and then northeast, until it reaches the Japanese coast. The warm, northeasterly flowing current between Formosa and latitude 35 degrees north is called the Kuroshio, Japanese for "Black Current." The Kuroshio Current is most similar in nature to the Florida Current, which travels the Caribbean Sea and crosses the Straits of Florida—in other words, the area of the Bermuda Triangle.

Although the storm systems and ocean currents of the Dragon Triangle are characteristically similar to those of the Bermuda Triangle, there are significant differences between their subsurface environments. The ocean floor below the surface of the Dragon Triangle is marked by much deeper trenches and ridges as well as considerably greater volcanic activity.

The deepest water on earth is in the Dragon Triangle. The depths of the Philippine Trench and the Japan Trench are estimated to exceed 10,000 meters. This "bottomless" ocean is certainly an unfathomable graveyard for countless ships and planes. Those which sink in these waters, especially when laden with heavy cargo, disappear into the depths, never to be found again. Unable to salvage or even locate lost ships, investigators have no clues as to the causes of the numerous shipping disasters or the fate of the crews.

A possible cause of these disasters is the underwater earthquake or volcanic explosion and the seiche wave, or *tsunami*, which it produces. When an earthquake occurs, its shock waves reverberate through the earth's crust. These vibrations travel up from the ocean floor in a column of water and manifest themselves on the surface in a series of waves rippling out from the source. The general term for this phenomenon is the seiche wave. In the Pacific Ocean, it is called the tsunami.

The tsunami (from the Japanese *tsu* for harbor, *nami* for wave) is a long, low wave on the open sea—about one foot in height. However, it can be 200 miles long and move at 500 miles per hour. For some reason, the tsunami travels in groups of up to six waves with about 100 miles between each one.

As these gain in amplitude in the shallows near the coastline, they become towering killers. Because of the relatively small size of the tsunami at sea, most ships are not damaged when struck by them. Some sailors have mistaken the dull thump of a tsunami hitting the sides as the ship hitting a rock or reef. This error has led to a number of nonexistent reefs showing up on navigational charts.

The tsunami is accompanied by a thunderlike roar. The novelist Joseph Conrad, himself a mariner, described a tsunami in *Lord Jim* as sounding as "if the thunder had growled deep down in the water." Many shipwreck survivors report having heard a similar noise immediately before their ships went down in the Dragon Triangle. This is puzzling, since the tsunami is most dangerous to islands and coastal cities. By the time the tsunami reaches a coastline, it has assumed tidal wave proportions and washes away anything it confronts.

However, individual waves of sufficient size can sink ships, even those as large and sophisticated as today's gargantuan cargo carriers. It is a scientific fact that winds above three miles an hour can wrinkle the ocean surface into ripples. Massive killer waves develop when the winds continue to work on them. In a stormy region such as the Dragon Triangle, large waves are an ever-present danger. Even more disconcerting to navigators is that waves of well over 100 feet in height have been known to appear suddenly among waves of lesser volume. A ship surprised by such a massive wall of water and unable to ride over it could be dispatched directly to the ocean bottom or spun in whirlpool fashion until water engulfed it.

It seems likely that many ships are lost in the Dragon Triangle because of wave damage. One of the most problematic and intriguing marine disasters involved the *Berge Istra*, popularly known as the "Green Giant" because of her huge 227,912 ton displacement. Shortly before the *Berge Istra* went down over the Mindanao Trench on December 29, 1975, her radio officer, Ronald Le Marche, contacted his wife in the British Channel Islands. He told her that the weather was good and the sea calm.

Out of the thirty crew members, only two survived, and those only because they were painting above decks when the ship began to sink. They swore they had heard explosions at the same time they had been blown off the ship into the sea.

Experts questioned this because no wreckage was ever found, as there would have been if the ship had blown up. Others have suggested that the *Berge Istra* was hijacked by Muslim extremists from Mindanao. This theory does not explain why the crewmen didn't realize they were being hijacked—or their insistence on the explosions.

There does not appear to be a plausible answer to the riddle. A tsunami, the result of underwater seismic activity, a giant wave born therein, or a distant storm may have struck the mammoth vessel and sent her directly to the bottom. The sound the survivors heard may not have been explosions but the tsunami's thunder. Because the tsunami does not accompany a storm, this would explain why the radio officer thought that the weather was good. No doubt the 188,000 tons of iron ore she was transporting acted as an anchor pulling her down once she had capsized. Or perhaps the weight of the cargo combined with the sudden battering by a series of tsunamis broke the *Berge Istra* in two and produced a sound which the crewmen mistook for an explosion. Nevertheless, a tsunami as we know it, large enough to capsize the Green Giant, would be rare indeed.

The ship's Norwegian owner, Sigvald Bergeson, was shocked by its disappearance and unable to explain the lack of communication before it went down. Bergeson maintained that the *Berge Istra* was only four years old and was equipped with the most modern safety devices and warning signals, to the extent that it was insured with Lloyds of London for $30 million.

An eerie sidelight to the *Berge Istra* incident is the disappearance of her sister ship, the *Berge Vanga*, three years and ten months later. The *Berge Vanga* was en route to Japan from South Africa when suddenly all radio contact was lost. No trace of wreckage was found and none of her forty-man crew survived. The two giant ships were owned by the same company, built in the same shipyards, carried the same cargo, and traveled the same routes—the sort of coincidence that makes legends.

The phenomenon of a ship splitting in two after a pummeling by waves or high winds is not uncommon. As marine disaster expert Richard Bishop put it, "If I had to guess what is the major cause for large ships going missing, I should unhesitatingly vote for massive fatigue cracking."

The ships most vulnerable to massive fatigue cracking are long, narrow ships, which are especially susceptible to splitting in half at the middle. Such an unfortunate event may have occurred in the cases of the *Berge Istra* and the *Berge Vanga*— and almost certainly happened to the *Derbyshire*.

The *Derbyshire* was a huge British ship weighing 169,044 tons. When it sank south of Tokyo Bay in September 1980, the entire forty-four-man crew was lost. There were no radio distress calls. Investigators confirmed that the *Derbyshire* was caught in a storm and theorized that it was broken in half by the waves. The disheartening reality that the very best of man's technology is no match for nature's power was bemoaned by Lord Campbell of Croy in the House of Lords. Once associated with the famous insurance company Lloyds of London, Lord Campbell warned that the government should "have something to say about how a production of modern shipyard technology can silently vanish in a noworse-than-average China Sea storm. . . ."

An intriguing sidelight to the disappearance of the *Derbyshire* involves a rumor that circulated before the tragedy. Although it was only four years old when it was lost, the *Derbyshire* had earned a reputation as an accident-prone jinx ship. One crew member, Peter Lambert, wrote to his mother in Liverpool and related that on the last trip, strange and unusual accidents had continued to occur. He told her that he would not sail on the *Derbyshire* again. Ironically, this prediction proved correct—and Lambert disappeared along with his fellow crewmen.

The *Derbyshire*'s demise may be similar to that of the Japanese ship *Bolivar (Boriba) Maru*. A 52,000 ton freighter carrying a heavy load of iron ore, the *Bolivar Maru* sank in high waves southeast of Tokyo Bay. Unlike the *Derbyshire*, two of the *Bolivar Maru*'s crew survived. One was a cook named Nakamura, the other the second engineer, Takaoba.

The radio officer managed to send two SOS messages to the Japanese coast guard. The first reported that the number two hatch was damaged and water was pouring into the hold. The second, relayed shortly before the ship sank, said that the bow was damaged as well.

Apparently neither the officers nor the crew were overly alarmed by the damage because they made no effort at speedy evacuation from the ship. Many of the sailors returned to their cabins where they changed their clothes and packed up their belongings. Second Engineer Takaoba was ordered by the first officer to collect official papers and gather food from breakfast to take into the lifeboats. Other crewmen stood by the lifeboats waiting for the command to lower them into the water.

"All of a sudden," Takaoba told the investigating team, "we heard a tremendous noise—'gishy-gishy'—the earthquake noise—and the ship started to break up and sink."

Takaoba jumped into the sea along with Nakamura, who was on another deck. When the *Takashima Maru*, a ship in the vicinity, arrived at the scene, it found the two men swimming in the area. No one else survived.

The special investigation committee assigned no blame to individuals. Instead, it surmised that the heavy cargo, structural problems, and bad weather sunk the ship. It is interesting to note the reference Takaoba made to the sound of the ship breaking up. It is reminiscent of the sound of explosions heard before the *Berge Istra* went down and may corroborate the theory that it sank after it split in two. The descriptive phrase, "the earthquake noise," certainly applies to the tsunami. Where would such a wave come from? Did it have to be large enough to capsize the ship or just strong enough to snap an already overladen cargo hold in two? Are mysterious tsunamis of killer proportions common in the Dragon Triangle?

The *California Maru*, another Japanese cargo ship, sank in Tokyo Bay just east of Chiba on February 10, 1970. Its bow had been damaged earlier off Nojima Zaki and, like the *Bolivar Maru*, when it began to fill with water, no one considered the situation desperate enough to take emergency steps. The *California Maru* continued blithely on its way, even though it was sailing under storm conditions.

The first engineer reported hearing a tremendous crunching sound and noticed that the ship had begun to list to port. Another crew member taking a bath at the time noticed that the water in the tub was spilling out the left side. Captain Sumimura stopped the *California Maru*'s engines and immediately summoned the twenty-two-man crew to their emergency positions on the bridge.

The crew lowered the lifeboats, but the waves were high and struck them. Some men were washed overboard and others were injured. Most of the survivors escaped by scrambling down Jacob's ladders and life nets to the New Zealand ship *Oteola*, which was standing by to rescue them. Luckily, there were Japanese crewmen aboard the *Oteola*, who were able to translate instructions. The captain of the *California Maru* was, however, unable to escape and went down with his ship.

The *California Maru* was the fourth large ship to sink off the Japanese coast in the space of a year. The *Bolivar Maru*, lost in March 1969, was the first. The *Sofia Pappas* disappeared on January 6, 1970, and the *Andrew Demades* went down two days later. All four sank during the worst winter months, when storms are the most frequent and deadly.

By studying the list of lost ships, certain groupings of disappearances by chronology and location become evident. For example, a number of ships went down between April 1949 and December 1954. The *Kuroshio Maru No. 1*, 1,525 tons, sank off the Bonin Islands on April 19, 1949. The precise location is unknown for its sister ship, *Kuroshio Maru No. 2*, which sank three days later. The 66-ton *Chōfuku Maru No. 5* disappeared on June 8, 1952, about 120 miles east of Okurajima, and the 500-ton *Kaiō Maru No. 5* on September 24. Two more ships were lost in June and December of 1953: the *Shinsei Maru*, 62 tons, went down off Sumisu Island in the Ogasawara Chain, while the 150-ton *Kōchi Maru No. 16* sank east of Iwo Jima. The year 1954 saw the demise of four more ships: the *Kuroshio Maru No. 3*, 1,525 tons, off Nishinoshima; the *Fuyō Maru No. 2*, 227 tons, off Miyakejima; the *Seisho Maru No. 1*, 190 tons, southeast of Okurajima; and the *Chiyo Maru No. 15*, 18 tons, near Kinansho.

The causes of the disappearances of each of the above ships are unknown. We do know that the relatively small size of these ships as evidenced by their light tonnage indicates that they were private or commercial fishing boats. In the years following World War II, the waters of the Dragon Triangle were traveled primarily by such boats.

Very few of these boats had radio transmitters or communication devices of any kind and so, when in trouble, they were not able to call for help. Even those equipped with transmitters sometimes found them untrustworthy. At the time that the *Kaiō Maru No. 5* disappeared during volcanic eruptions near the Myojinsho Reef, the 150 ton *Toshi Maru* was reported missing in the same area and presumed to have suffered the same fate. The ship was discovered in late September 1952 and the captain reported that its radio transmitter had failed!

Yet even in more recent times, well-equipped vessels with all sorts of technological aids have disappeared without a trace, or encountered mysterious disasters. In January of 1970, the Liberian freighter *Sophia Pappas* broke in two and vanished in the waters southeast of Tokyo Bay. The sixteen-year-old, 12,113-ton vessel had a crew of twenty-nine—only twenty-two of whom were rescued. Another Liberian vessel, the 13,616-ton *Banaluna*, disappeared en route to Kokura with a 2,846-ton load of magnetite. The ship's last message was sent on November 12, 1971. Despite an extensive search no traces of either the vessel or its thirty-five-man crew were ever found.

In February of 1977, a Panamanian-registered vessel, the *Triumph No. 1*, disappeared appproximately 480 miles off the coast of Japan. The question remains—how could an 8,342-ton vessel simply sink without a trace? Then there is the case of the Greek freighter *Agios Giorgis*, a 16,565-ton vessel carrying 25,000 tons of scrap steel to Mizushima. Instead, it sank off Inubo Saki, with a loss of all twenty-nine hands aboard. No SOS was ever sent.

Perhaps transmitter breakdown is the reason the 102,805-ton cargo ship *Hae Dang Wha* never called for help before it sank on July 28, 1980. Loaded with iron ore, the *Hae Dang Wha* vanished somewhere over the northern Mindanao Trench while en route from Japan to Korea. Her last message reported clear sailing and no inclement weather or operational difficulties. Why had a ship valued at $2.6 million disappeared, taking all twenty-nine hands with her? Fifteen days of intensive search operations failed to find any trace of the *Hae Dang Wha*, and she was declared "missing with all hands; cause unknown."

Some investigators have tried to grapple with the numerous

The 8,198-ton Liberian *Sophia Pappas* broke in two southeast of Tokyo Bay on January 5, 1970. (*Photo from the Author's Collection*)

The 13,616-ton Liberian *Banaluna* was bound for Kokura, Japan, and carried 2,846 tons of magnetite when it disappeared along with its thirty-five crewmembers. Its last radio message on November 12, 1971, indicated no alarm, and even after extensive searches not a trace was found. (*Photo from the Author's Collection*)

The Panamanian *Triumph No. 1* vanished 480 miles off the coast of Japan on February 22, 1977. Neither the 8,342-ton ship nor any of the crewmembers were ever located. (*Photo from the Author's Collection*)

Carrying 25,000 tons of scrap steel and weighing 16,565 tons, the Greek ship *Agios Giorgis* fell prey to the Dragon Triangle on January 8, 1970. Neither its twenty-nine crewmembers nor any wreckage was ever found. (*Photo from the Author's Collection*)

unexplained marine disasters in the Dragon Triangle. One explanation may be that some unscrupulous ship owners pay to have their property destroyed in order to collect insurance money. A number of the smaller vessels were twenty to twenty-five years old and were transporting valuable cargoes of electronics, tin, or textiles when they sank.

In some instances, investigators were able to prove that certain crewmen showed up repeatedly on vessels which sank, leading to the conclusion that they were paid to scuttle them. During a court trial involving the *Jal Sea Condor*, a Hong Kong judge characterized the captain and chief engineer of the 7,000 ton cargo vessel as "venal scoundrels whose prime concern was to receive a substantial reward" from the insurance company.

Like the waters of the Bermuda Triangle, the Dragon Triangle has been plagued by sea raiders, hijackers—and pirates. The China coast has historically been a haven for seafaring plunderers. At one time there were more than 300 pirate junks terrorizing the waters of the Dragon Triangle. Many unhappy ships sailing close to the coast found themselves surrounded and attacked by these pirates, who made quick sorties out from the thousands of inlets, coves, and tiny islands. Known as the Red Flag Fleet, this criminal flotilla boasted a force of between 20,000 and 40,000 men. One of the most deadly, and most romantic, was the female pirate Shih Hsiang-Ku. Her fame as a murderous, thoroughly ruthless brigand gave rise to the appellation Dragon Lady. Her story and character were immortalized in the person of the Chinese pirate chieftainess in Milton Caniff's *Terry and the Pirates* comic strip. Much to the relief of the navigators in the area, Shih Hsiang-Ku was finally captured and executed on November 16, 1807.

Sometimes pirates would sail as passengers on a ship, or even sign on as crew. Then, at a given time and place, they would take over the unlucky vessel, murder the captain and crew, and make off with the ship and its cargo. Those ships most vulnerable to this type of assault were the smaller ones with only a few crew members. The ship would then be disposed of or altered in such a way as to conceal its original identity and used again. If the superstructure were sufficiently modified, the coast guard would not be able to recognize the pirated ship. The owners would report the ship lost without a trace and, if possible, collect the insurance.

There are other reasons ships have vanished in the Dragon Triangle and elsewhere. On-board fires and explosions, especially in the engine room, have caused enough damage to send a ship to the bottom. These could be the result of mechanical or electrical malfunctions within the ship itself, or caused by the mysterious electromagnetic anomalies known to exist in the Dragon Triangle.

In rough seas, cargo has been known to shift in the hold. This sudden redistribution of weight can force a ship to list to one side and take on water. Many of the ships that vanished in this area were carrying extremely heavy cargoes which, if dislodged in a storm, could easily sink ships, if not snap them in half. Doubtless this may be a contributing factor in some of the disappearances of the supercargo ships.

In rare instances, ships have sunk after striking a submerged object. This could be a reef, floating mine, or previously sunken ship lying just below the surface of the water. In the Pacific Ocean, coral grows along the sides of extinct volcanoes. A reef slowly forms as millions of skeletons of coral polyps pile up. Gradually, the volcano will wear away and sink back into the ocean floor, leaving the coral at its original level. These coral atolls, as they are called, are often found at the tips of volcanic islands and can pose a significant hazard to shipping. They are well charted and known to sailors in the area. The Dragon Triangle, however, with its frequent seismic upthrusts and subsidences, sometimes turns reliable charts into deadly guessing games.

The waters of the Pacific Basin, especially the Philippine and Japan seas, were the scenes of many naval battles and intense military activity during World War II. As soon as the peace treaty with Japan was signed on September 2, 1945, Allied minesweepers began to clear the mines from the area. The task was performed in three phases. First, the channels into Japanese-held ports were swept so that Allied prisoners of war could be evacuated and occupation forces landed. Second, the harbors and channels were opened so that supplies could be brought in. The last were the sea lanes.

After the war, all ocean traffic was in danger from mines, and no ships could enter Japanese waters until the waters had been swept. British, Dutch, and Australian sweepers cleared the islands south of the Philippines and the Asiatic coast. The American YMSs, or small minesweepers, cleared the Philippines, Palaus, Marshalls, Gilberts, and Bonins. The Russians were responsible for the Manchurian coast.

This was no small job. The coasts of China, Southeast Asia, Singapore, Borneo, New Guinea, Korea, Japan, Manila, and the islands and sea lanes of the Philippine Sea had been seeded with deadly mines. Allied and Japanese mines laid by aircraft, submarines, and surface vessels now had to be lifted.

Tokyo Bay had seventy-four Japanese contact mines and three belonging to the United States. Over a 164-mile area at Kagoshima, there were 320 mines. Kōchi was blocked by 212. Sasebo was dotted with 1,200 mines and the area was declared clean in October 1945. Ten days later, a Japanese ship sank there. The reason? It struck a mine.

The channel between Kōchi and Kyushu, Bungo Suidō, contained 3,400 mines. The American minesweeper lifted 1,687 and the Japanese 222, and yet the channel was considered only partially safe. In Nagoya, many magnetic mines laid by American submarines and Japanese forces were never found, even though sweepers spent 1,900 minesweeper days looking for them. And these represented only the mines just near the coast of Japan.

Eight American ships struck mines during the sweeping operations but only one sank. The *Minivet* went down on December 29, 1945, and one officer and thirty crew men drowned. In November, the Japanese ship *Daito Maru* sank off Tsushima after running into a mine.

The Japanese estimated they had laid 51,400 mines from Formosa up through the Tsugaru and La Perouse straits. At least 39,000 mines went unswept. Many broke their moorings and drifted with the currents. At the beginning of World War II, the Japanese had attached a disarming device to these mines that would deactivate the mines should they break cable. However, as the war drew to a close, the Japanese ceased to use these devices—they were not manufactured well and the Japanese had too many other problems to deal with. Fully 50 percent of all Japanese moored mines were estimated to be live and dangerous after breaking their moorings.

The most dangerous underwater perils were the pressure mines. They floated just below the surface of the ocean and were set off when the water pressure changed as a large ship passed overhead. When the Russians were sweeping the China coast and Korea, they asked the Americans for advice on how to clear pressure mines. Admiral Sharp, the officer in charge of the minesweeping operation, responded honestly that he didn't know. In fact, the only effective way was to trigger the pressure mine by sailing a large ship over it. This is a very expensive method and so the Americans decided to allow the mines to grow old and neutralize themselves.

No matter how old, live floating mines are always dangerous. By July 1948, 251 ships of all nationalities had hit mines in the Atlantic and Pacific oceans. Of those, 116 sank or were totally wrecked. It is probable that some of the thousands of explosive mines unaccounted for are still adrift in the area of the Dragon Triangle where so many were originally placed. Therefore, although the chances are small, it is possible that one or two of the lost ships exploded upon striking one of the mines.

Even more remote but theoretically possible is the phenomenon of a submerged shipwreck suddenly rising to the surface or just below. Acting as a kind of man-made reef, it would pose a serious threat to any unsuspecting vessel which might strike it. Although we have no recorded instances of ships in the Dragon Triangle actually running into such ghost ships, perhaps this explains a few of the many that have sunk without a trace.

A considerable amount of research has been undertaken within the last few years in order to ascertain why great ships in an age of high technology, satellite navigation, and improved communication can still vanish, as Francis Cooper, a marine writer, has expressed it, "as magically and completely as if they had sailed off the earth."

The Dragon Triangle has experienced more than its share of mysterious and unexplained shipping disasters. Even taking into account the unusual volcanic activity and proclivity for sudden violent storms which produce deadly tidal waves, too many ships are unaccounted for. It almost seems that there is a ghost *tsunami* traversing the Triangle giving its victims a warning in the form of a thundering roar. Too many men have heard it. Too many radios have failed in the critical minutes, and too few lost ships have been found to give witness to their fate.

The atmospheric, oceanographic, and seismic characteristics of the Dragon Triangle make it truly seem to be a dragon's lair—a dangerous place to sail and a merciless trap for its unwary victims.

4

Planes That Never Landed

World War II certainly instituted the beginning of heavy-volume air traffic through the Dragon Triangle, namely, the Allied bomber offensive against Japan. This did not begin until 1944, as the Allied forces lacked very-long-range (VLR) bombers which could carry the necessary heavy loads of explosives over 3,000 miles. With the development of the B-29 Superfortress, the Allies finally had the necessary delivery system. However, these planes were so newly developed that operational problems plagued the bomber offensive.

The initial plan was to use the B-29s at 30,000 feet. However, the high winds encountered at those altitudes, plus problems with ice on instruments and engines, increased losses for the months after the first raid in June of 1944. The bombers were first based in eastern China, and their attacks were so successful that the Japanese forces were stung into a major offensive to destroy the air bases. While the Japanese succeeded in their goal, American forces seized new bases in the Mariana Islands. Soon twenty bombardment groups based on Saipan and Tinian flew day and night over Japan, gutting thirty-two square miles of cities.

It is interesting to note that Tinian and Saipan mark one of the corners of the Dragon Triangle. We will never know if the strange phenomena of the Triangle are responsible for Allied losses, since they would be lost in the statistics of operational problems and enemy activity. However, another strange sidelight to this major wartime operation is the phenomenon known as the foo fighters—mysterious balls of light that followed Allied bombers along their routes to Japan. (See Chapter 8.)

The Allied bomber offensive is also definitely responsible for one wartime aeronautic mystery of the Dragon Triangle. Allied B-29s needed fighter cover for their sorties, which meant taking a base nearer to the Japanese home islands. The only choice was Iwo Jima, a heavily defended island with three airstrips and 22,000 troops. At least fifty Japanese planes were lost in the fighting, mainly through kamikaze tactics. However, before the battle actually began, one Japanese plane mysteriously disappeared.

Just as the Americans used Catalina flying boats for patrol and antisubmarine duties, the Imperial Japanese forces used the Kawanishi HK-8 flying boat to scout the skies. One such plane was in the air near Iwo Jima, on patrol. In those final days of the war, the Allies often held air superiority, despite Japanese raids. American bombers had already attacked the Iwo Jima airstrips as part of the softening up process for an invasion. The flying boat stood ready to report any intruders into the island's airspace.

However, when the Kawanishi's commander contacted his base, he sent an unusual spoken message. Shiro Kawamoto, the commander of a Zero flight wing, still remembered the strange message years after the war ended. At the time he received it he thought the message was peculiar, for it did not refer to enemy activities but to something that the pilot of the Kawanishi was himself experiencing. His voice sounded confused and uncertain as he reported, "Something is happening to the sky . . . the sky is opening up—." Here the message abruptly ended.

Although U.S. forces were poised for an attack on Iwo Jima, there were no attacks from either side on the night of the Kawanishi incident. The report, with its indication of something highly unusual happening in the sky overhead, was never explained—nor was the plane, pilot, or crew ever found. A number of other air disappearances have since occurred over or approaching the Dragon Triangle, but they happened in peacetime and generally under good weather conditions.

In both the Bermuda and the Dragon triangles, small boats engaging in smuggling operations often appear and disappear as a matter of convenience. A boat will disappear either through hijacking or false report and then reappear with changed superstructure so that it will not be recognized by coast guard cutters.

The drug trade in the Dragon Triangle is not so profitable or widespread as it used to be before the death penalty for a second conviction for drug use or sale was instituted in mainland China. In the Bermuda Triangle, however, smuggling of drugs by surface craft is a thriving industry increasingly difficult to control.

Drug smuggling by air may account for a considerable number of light aircraft being found under the shallow waters around the Bahamas. The unusual aspect of this wreckage is that the planes have *not* been reported missing. Their wreckage near airfields or in shallow waters is there for all to see. Occasionally an unidentified wrecked plane has to be dragged off an airfield where it had landed when no one saw it, at an hour when the airfield was closed.

The explanation for this anomaly is easy to understand. Drug smugglers fly the cargo from Colombia, for example, and transfer it to a fast power boat for easy delivery to the extensive keys and backwaters of South Florida. The aircraft is sunk or wrecked or simply abandoned—a matter of little consequence to the drug smugglers, considering the value of the transferred cargo.

But the aircraft that have disappeared in the Dragon Triangle are not engaged in smuggling. They have included large military planes carrying numerous personnel, as well as planes searching for the large cargo ships that have disappeared in the area. These planes have vanished while flying missions in clear skies and good flying weather. Communication with some of the planes that later disappeared indicated nothing untoward about the sky, the sea, the weather, or the functioning of the aircraft.

On March 12, 1957, a KB-50 (the tanker version of the B-29) with a crew of eight disappeared in good weather on a flight between Japan and Wake Island. There were no distress signals, and air investigation found no trace of the plane or its crew. A U.S. Navy JD-1 Invader disappeared on a routine flight between Japan and Okinawa on March 16, 1957. Weather conditions were normal. No SOS was received. No wreckage or crew members were found after an extensive search. On March 22, 1957, a C-97 U.S. military transport with sixty-seven military personnel aboard disappeared southeast of Japan while beginning its landing approach. The last radio message was 200 miles from Tokyo, indicating that all was well and flying conditions good. There was no further message—then or ever. A nine-day air-sea search and rescue mission was initiated over thousands of square miles of ocean surface. However, it yielded no trace of the C-97, the passengers, or the crew.

It is notable that these three planes vanished within nine days of one another, constituting a collective peacetime air tragedy comparable to one of the most famous Bermuda Triangle mysteries, the disappearance of Flight 19.

On December 5, 1945, the five Avenger torpedo bombers of Flight 19 left the Fort Lauderdale, Florida, naval air station on a routine navigation exercise. Fourteen navy and marine airmen took off and were never seen again. Two hours into the flight, Lieutenant Charles C. Taylor, the squadron's commander, radioed the Fort Lauderdale control tower with an emergency announcement that the entire flight was lost. Despite the fact that flying conditions were fair to good, Taylor radioed, "Everything is wrong . . . strange. We can't be sure of any direction. Even the ocean doesn't look as it should." Within half an hour, radio contact had ceased.

A rescue plane, a Martin Mariner PBM flying boat, headed for the last estimated position of Flight 19. The plane, with its thirteen-man crew, reported reaching the position, and gave one further position check. Then it too disappeared. Six planes and twenty-seven men had vanished, in the words of one naval officer, "as if they'd flown to Mars."

While the Dragon Triangle's 1957 tragedy took only three planes, it accounted for the lives of eighty personnel. The period of the three disappearances near Japan has been referred to as the nightmare month of aviation.

During this same period, on March 19, 1957, President Ramon Magsaysay of the Philippines, with twenty-four staff and crew members, disappeared in a flight near Cebu, suggesting the possibility that an air aberration or skyquake had affected an extensive area along the great oceanic trenches from Japan to the Philippines. Again, an intensive search revealed no survivors.

Other planes disappeared both before and after the night-mare month in the Dragon Triangle. These included the loss of a USAF F-3B twin engine all-weather fighter. The jet left Atsugi Air Force Base and after attaining an altitude of 15,000 feet it vanished. An immediate massive search by several hundred planes and ships revealed no trace of the missing jet. Other losses close to base included a Japanese Marine Defense P2V-7, an antisubmarine patrol plane with a 101-foot wing-span. This aircraft took off with a crew of eight on April 27, 1971, for a night training flight. Turning back because of unfavorable weather, it radioed for permission to land. The plane never landed and was never found. Two months later, on June 23, a single-pilot training IM-1 vanished in the Dragon Triangle with no findings on the part of the investigating board as to what happened.

A USAF C-130 disappeared twenty miles southwest of Okinawa with a crew of nine on April 10, 1970. (A C-130 and a KB-50 are also counted among the planes lost in the Bermuda Triangle.)

Among the smaller planes which have disappeared in the Dragon Triangle is the JA-341, another case similar to the fate of the rescue plane which disappeared searching for the Lost Squadron. The JA-341 vanished while covering the sinking of the *California Maru* for the press. It is almost as though certain areas of the ocean, because of weather, tectonic activity, or other reasons, become extremely dangerous at certain times. This not only imperils ships and planes, but also puts the craft sent to their rescue at risk.

In the early days of aviation, pilots often flew "by the seat of their pants," with minimal reliance on primitive chronom-eters or easily disrupted gyrocompasses. When flying over the vast distances of the Pacific, with small islands as landing targets, this approach could easily bring disaster. However, today's larger, faster jets, with their supersophisticated locational controls, leave the pilot at the mercy of his machinery—with disaster to follow if these instruments prove unreliable.

Consider the case of KAL Flight 007, a Korean airliner returning home on September 11, 1983, from across the Pacific. Although it was superbly equipped for navigation with VOR, ADF, Omega, and LORAN, it strayed off course on its homeward journey, infringing on Soviet airspace. The results were fatal. Soviet aircraft shot the plane down with a loss of life of 269 passengers and crew. The Soviets admitted the attack, which they considered justifiable, as KAL 007 was considered automatically a potential enemy aircraft or, at the very least, a spy plane flying through a restricted zone.

The reason the pilot crossed into the USSR may be connected to compass malfunction and failure to immediately check further controls. It is well known that compasses in certain areas are affected by isogonic force lines between the poles, so that pilots must adjust their compass readings to establish true north and south along the course they are flying. The areas of the Bermuda and Dragon triangles, alike in so many other physical aberrations, magnetic irregularities, and seismic and volcanic activity, are also alike in the changing paths of the isogonic lines. It is possible that the tragedy of KAL 007 was caused by a temporary magnetic shift, noticed by many pilots in both triangles. In this case, however, the shift took place too close to the wrong border.

Another pilot to encounter the danger of instrument dependence was the late entertainer Arthur Godfrey, a well-known amateur pilot. While flying his own twin-engine jet on a world tour, he encountered an electronic aberration east of Japan—in the Dragon Triangle. His flight instruments, including the compasses, the gas gauge, and even the radio, abruptly went dead. With gas for only three hours of flight on hand, Godfrey navigated as well as he could by the sun. After an hour, the instruments suddenly began to operate again, as inexplicably as they had stopped. Godfrey found he was not only far off course, but, comparing watch time with radio time, he had lost half an hour. Perhaps this time-shift can also explain the experience of a pilot who reported a strange anomaly to Ivan Sanderson when that author was plotting major areas of mysterious disappearances. On a flight to Guam in an ancient propeller-driven plane, this pilot covered 340 miles in one hour—about 200 miles farther than the plane's capabilities—with no winds to assist.

Other pilots besides Arthur Godfrey have experienced a complete radio blackout zone in the Dragon Triangle. This blind spot has lasted as long as one and one-half hours, at which point the instruments suddenly started functioning again.

A more universal problem may also explain some of the aircraft losses in recent years—wind shear. Although the aeronautics industry has been aware of the dangers of heavy downdrafts of air for years, it is only since 1975 that the general public has encountered the term *wind shear*. On June 24 of that year, an Eastern Airlines Boeing 727 making a landing at John F. Kennedy Airport in New York came down disastrously short of Runway 22L—nearly 2,400 feet short, resulting in the loss of 112 lives among the 124 aboard the plane.

The term gained wider currency with the crash of a Pan American 727 shortly after taking off from the New Orleans airport on July 9, 1982. The death toll was 159, with 9 injured. Eight of the fatalities were on the ground in a residential neighborhood.

In 1985, the crash of a Delta L-1011 jetliner at the Dallas–Fort Worth airport brought "wind shear" to a new national prominence, to the point where media people are sure to ask if the phenomenon is responsible for any aeronautic disaster.

Essentially, a wind shear is a sudden blast of air on the vertical axis, an up or down crosswind, one might say. The well-known meteorologist Dr. Tetsuya Theodore Fujita began to study the phenomenon after he noticed strange patterns in the aerial photographs depicting downed trees from the superoutbreak tornadoes near Beckley, West Virginia, in April of 1974. In some photos, instead of the swirling patterns usually found from tornadoes, hundreds of trees were blown down and outward, in a starburst pattern. Trees near the center of the starburst were flattened or uprooted, and spattered with topsoil. The evidence argued that a violent jet of wind landed hard in the midst of the starburst, bounced off the ground, then scattered outward on a horizontal axis.

Using this model, Dr. Fujita undertook to explain the Eastern Airlines crash of 1975. The 727 had encountered a similar wind starburst, which literally blew it to the ground. The winds were strong enough to divert a jet aircraft in flight, yet so localized that they were not detected by any of the airport's ground-based anemometers. Dr. Fujita called the phenomenon the *downburst*, and further developed a gradation of sizes—the *macroburst*, whose winds extend more than two and a half miles, move as fast as 134 miles per hour, and cause widespread, tornadolike damage, and the *microburst*, whose winds extend only within a two-and-a-half-mile zone, but are more powerful (as high as 168 miles an hour).

Dr. Fujita attributes the cause of these downbursts to cyclonic winds; however, unlike a tornado, whose wind funnel stays more or less vertical to the earth's surface, downburst wind vortices stay horizontal to the surface. They start out as a torus ring or doughnut of swirling air, dragging air downward from the sky as tempestuous vertical winds. As the vortex torus expands, it finally breaks up, sending off fragments like gigantic, invisible steamrollers to cause further destruction.

Wind shear had originally been connected only with the air convection currents of thunderstorms. In field studies during 1978 and 1982, Dr. Fujita proved the existence of both wet and dry downbursts. In an eighty-six-day period at Denver's Stapleton Airport, the investigators' radar pinpointed 155 dry microbursts, 83 percent of the total 186 bursts discovered. This means that a low-flying plane could encounter fair weather and still be hurled from the sky at great speed.

Exactly how swiftly a wind shear downburst can affect a plane is illustrated in this transcript from the flight recorder on the doomed Delta Flight 191 to Dallas–Fort Worth. It is important to note that the crew was aware of thunderstorms in the area and was on guard. (Conversation inside the cockpit is italicized.)

Delta 191 First Officer: *We're going to get our airplane washed.*

Delta 191 Captain: *What?*

Delta 191 First Officer: *We're going to get our airplane washed.*

Delta 191 Captain: Approach, Delta 191 with you at 5.

Approach Control: 191 heavy, expect 17 left.

Delta 191 First Officer: Thank you, sir.

Approach Control: Delta 191 heavy, fly heading of 350.

Delta 191 Captain: Roger.

Approach Control: American 351, do you see the runway yet?

American 351: As soon as we break out of this rain shower we will.

Approach Control: Okay 351, you're 4 from the marker, join the localizer at or above 2,300 cleared for ILS 17 left approach.

American 351: Cleared for the ILS, American 351.

Approach Control: 191 heavy, reduce speed 170, turn left 270.

Delta 191 Captain: Roger.

Approach Control: Five Juliet Foxtrot, turn left 190.

5JF: Left turn 190.

Approach Control: Five Juliet Foxtrot, increase your speed to 170 knots, hold that to marker, you're 5 miles from the marker, join the localizer at or above 3,000, cleared for an ILS 17 left approach.

5JF: Cleared for the 17 left approach, roger, we're around to 190.

Approach Control: Delta 191 heavy, turn left 240, descend and maintain 3,000.

Delta 191 Captain: 191, 240, out of 5 for 3.

Approach Control: American 351, tower 126.55.

American 351: So long.

Approach Control: November 5 Juliet Foxtrot is 4 miles from the marker, maintain a speed of 170 or better to the marker, you're cleared ILS 17 left, contact tower 126.55.

5JF: 126.95, good day.

Approach Control: That's 126.55.

5JF: 26.55, good day.

Approach Control: Delta 191 heavy is 6 miles from the marker, turn left heading 180, join the localizer at or above 2,300, cleared for the ILS 17 left approach.

Delta 191 Captain: Delta 191, roger all that, appreciate it.

Approach Control: Delta 191 heavy, reduce your speed to 160 please.

Delta 191 Captain: Be glad to.

Delta 191 Captain: *160.*

Delta 191 First Officer: *All right.*

Delta 191 Captain: Localizer and glideslope captured . . . 160 is your speed.

Approach Control: And we're getting some variable winds out there due to a shower on short out there north end of D/FW.

Unidentified Delta 191 Crewmember: *Stuff is moving in . . .*

Delta 191 Captain: *160's the speed.*

Approach Control: Delta 191 heavy, reduce speed to 150, contact tower 126.55.

Delta 191 Captain: 126.55, you have a nice day, we appreciate the help.

Delta 191 Captain: Tower, Delta 191 heavy, out here in the rain, feels good.

Tower: Delta 191 heavy, regional tower, 17 left, cleared to land, wind 090 at 5, gusts to 15.

Delta 191 Captain: Thank you, sir.

Tower: American 351, if you can make that next high speed there, pull up behind Delta and hold short of 17 right this frequency. [This transmission was to the American Airlines flight that had just landed on Runway 17.]

American 351: 351.

Delta 191 First Officer: *Lightning coming out of that one.*

Delta 191 Captain: *Where?*

Delta 191 First Officer: *Right ahead of us.*

Delta 191 Flight Engineer: *You've got good legs, don't you.*

Delta 191 Captain: *A thousand feet . . . 762 in the baro- . . . I'll call them out for you.*

Delta 191 First Officer: *All right.*

Delta 191 Captain: *Watch your speed . . . you're going to lose it all of a sudden, there it is . . . push it up, push it way up . . . way up . . . way up . . . that's it . . . hang on to the [profanity].*

Ground Proximity Warning System: Whoop, whoop, pull up.

Tower: November 15 Juliet Foxtrot can you make the, ah, we'll expedite down to the, ah, taxi 31, and a right turn off the traffic's a mile final. [These instructions were to the business jet that had just landed.]

The ground proximity warning system aboard the Delta airline continued to sound. One impact was recorded, followed by another. The tower tried to tell the airliner to go around for another approach, but it had already begun to crash. The onset of the catastrophe was so quick that there are only four lines of response by the crew on the transcript, about ten seconds' time—insufficient to avoid disaster.

Dr. Fujita's research has proven that downbursts are dangerous not merely for aircraft, but also for surface vessels. In his book, *The Downburst: Microburst and Macroburst*, Dr. Fujita records the capsizing of a sternwheeler steamboat due to a microburst downdraft. The episode took place on the Tennessee River near Ditto Landing on July 7, 1984.

The double-decked boat was 92 feet long, 20 feet wide, and 25 feet high, with 18 people on board. At 11:20 A.M. a thunderstorm began, accompanied by high winds from the west, which became stronger and stronger in a matter of minutes, until they were in the range of 57 to 67 miles per hour, a whole gale almost of hurricane proportions. The captain turned the ship into the wind, when suddenly the wind seemed to shift by 90 degrees. A strong gust struck the sternwheeler on the left side, and it capsized. Eleven people lost their lives, and two more were injured.

A recording anemometer nearby caught a reading of seventy-mile-an-hour winds at the time, though this was due to another microburst landing in its vicinity. By charting wind damage on a map, Dr. Fujita determined the directions of the winds, and found that while the entire storm was a macroburst site, three microbursts had descended on the area as well. As the captain turned his ship to face the high winds of the macroburst, a microburst downdraft developed to the south of his position. The expanding vortex ring is probably what capsized the boat.

The wind shear phenomenon is not limited to the area near the earth's surface. It has been experienced quite high in the air as well. In the days of propeller-driven aircraft, there had been the theory that if one flew high enough, it would be possible to avoid weather or turbulence. As high-altitude operations became the norm with jet planes, it was discovered that the air does not become smoother—and that turbulence could exist even in clear air.

Clear air turbulence, or CAT, was officially defined in 1966 by the National Committee for Clear Air Turbulence as "all turbulence in the free atmosphere of interest in aerospace operations that is not in, or adjacent to, visible convective activity [cumulus clouds]. This includes turbulence found in cirrus clouds, not in or adjacent to visible convective activity."

In layman's language, this means that CAT is all turbulence not connected with the spinning winds of cumulus storm clouds (which are notorious for spawning tornadoes).

Air disturbances also take place in clear air, or in thin, fair-weather cirrus clouds. This wind shear can be felt as sudden up- or downdrafts, which can throw an aircraft into a bumpy ride. Since pilots have no warning of this occurrence, the unexpected jolt to their craft can lead to considerable danger.

As with downbursts, CAT can extend in patches of only a few kilometers in diameter, with anything from a few hundred to a few thousand feet in depth. Oddly enough, the larger patches of turbulence are thought to be safer than smaller ones, as the larger wind gusts are experienced by a plane much more gradually, giving the craft more time to ride them out. A slow plane will experience much less CAT than a fast one, and a heavy plane will ride turbulence more smoothly than a small one. Planes with flexible wings will experience less turbulence than planes with rigid wings. However, CAT still exacts its price, for continued flexing will result in material fatigue, shortening the aircraft's useful life.

Clear air turbulence is usually linked to the jet streams, those enormous, three-dimensional rivers of air which form between the tropical and polar weather fronts. High in the sky—between 20,000 and 35,000 feet—they were only discovered during the high-altitude bombing of World War II. Pilots today use them as super tailwinds to add up to 400 miles per hour to their flight speed. As with all currents—air or water—eddies develop, spinning off from simple friction. Where there is a core of very high wind speeds, the eddies will be very strong and very turbulent. CAT occurs mainly near thermally stable atmospheric layers in the stratosphere, where warm air strata float on top of cold air. Its wind shear causes the usually laminar flow between the air masses to break up into eddies of all sizes.

An interesting thing to note about clear air turbulence is that it is invisible and fairly small in scale, so that planes can pass nearby and not even be aware of it. Large planes can move through areas of CAT and hardly notice, while slow-moving planes or subsonic jets may not experience a bumpy ride because they move over the waves or eddies smoothly.

The greatest danger is for relatively small, fast-moving aircraft like military fighters and bombers, which constitute a major portion of the planes that have vanished in the Dragon Triangle. Could a massive wind shear have struck them out of the lonely skies like some sort of cosmic hammer? It is a tantalizing possibility—and for travelers, an unpleasant one.

The upper-atmospheric reaches of the stratosphere represent one of mankind's great remaining frontiers—one right on the edge of space and perhaps receiving some very unpleasant visitors from beyond.

The near-Earth orbital belt is filled with numerous satellites, some of them up there for more than twenty years. Inevitably some orbits decay, and the resulting space junk plummets to Earth, creating a new and unforeseen danger for those who fly the high skies.

Still another unforeseen danger may well be the technical prowess of which we are so proud. Imagine the effect of a massive downburst on an aircraft whose electrical systems have suddenly become nonfunctional—a not uncommon problem in the Dragon and Bermuda triangles. For pilots flying virtually blind, it could mean the end. And the planes would be hurtled deep into the water at high speeds, to sink without a trace. It is a compelling scenario.

New technological aids are under development to warn pilots of wind shears; Doppler radar will even be able to scan for winds. However, this high technology is only as dependable as its power source. And the leading edge of aeronautic technology, the "fly-by-wire" concept, where the rudder and ailerons will be controlled by electric motors tied into a flight computer, could prove catastrophic in regions where electromagnetic anomalies can wipe out all instruments. In a moment, a supermodern aircraft would be turned into a hulk, blind, deaf, dumb, and paralyzed, soon to plummet to the ground—or sea.

In discussing the future of supersonic transport planes, meteorologists and aeronautical engineers have been reminded that clear air turbulence and wind shear can be expected to exist at the levels where these new aircraft will operate. Consideration must be given in terms of design and the possible effects on engine performance.

It might be well for these scientists and engineers to give consideration to areas nearer to Earth than those lofty altitudes—to areas like the Dragon Triangle. In no other part of the world except the Bermuda Triangle do so many unexplained disappearances take place, while at the same time more usual shipwrecks and sinkings are regularly reported.

In mapping the number of downburst aeronautic incidents for his book, Dr. Fujita noted that the vast majority took place in the United States. This was not necessarily due to a greater frequency of downbursts in that part of the world, he explained, but simply because the frequency of landings and takeoffs allowed him to isolate and study the phenomenon.

It is possible that even parts of the world regularly traveled by ships and planes can still hold strange phenomena that we cannot begin to understand or which science is still not ready to accept.

These mysteries may be connected not only with our own electronic devices and their malfunction, but with the forces of the earth itself, magnified by the swirling tides and currents of the ocean, and indeed, of the atmosphere itself. Despite our modern superships and airplanes, their scientific controls, safety devices, and improved communications systems, we still sail the seas and skies with some of the same uncertainty as in the days of legend.

5

Submarines That Never Surfaced

Surface vessels are not the only victims of the Dragon Triangle: a number of Soviet submarines have vanished as a result of the forces that operate in the deep waters off the coast of Japan and its offshore islands. These incidents have occurred in peacetime, and information on them would probably not be so openly available except for the Euro-Atomic Nuclear Safety Organization, an agency of the United Nations located in Brussels.

Signatories to the Nuclear Safety Agreement are pledged to report whenever their submarines, surface ships, or aircraft lose a nuclear reactor or nuclear weapon. In the case of the Soviet submarines, which were patrolling the ocean near Japan, this stipulation was followed and the losses reported.

The Nuclear Safety Agreement, however, does not specify that all details of the loss be given. In some cases, it has been impossible to determine the reasons for the submarine disappearances, as the only evidence is beyond the reach of investigators. We must take the reasonable supposition, however, that some of the lost submersibles were nuclear armed, although this information has evidently not yet attained *perestroika* status.

The following Soviet submarines have sunk or vanished near the coast of Japan, usually from causes not revealed:

Date of Disappearance	Class	Type	Location	Casualties
April 1968	Golf	Diesel/ electric powered	Northwest of Japan	86 dead
1970	Alfa	Nuclear powered	Sea of Japan	Exact number of dead and survivors unknown
1971	Yankee	Nuclear powered	Near Guam	Crew numbers unknown; no survivors
September 1974	Golf II	Diesel/ electric powered	Southwest of Japan	No survivors
November 1976	Foxtrot	Diesel/ electric powered	Sea of Japan	Unknown
1977	Unidentified	Nuclear powered	South China Sea	Exact numbers unknown

Date of Disappearance	Class	Type	Location	Casualties
August 1980	Echo I	Nuclear powered	Sea of Japan	Exact numbers unknown
October 1981	Whiskey	Diesel/ electric powered	Northwest of Japan	Unknown
September 1983	Charlie	Nuclear powered	Sea of Japan	90 dead
March 1984	Victor I	Nuclear powered	West of Japan	Unknown
September 1984	Echo II	Nuclear powered	60 miles west of Japan	Unknown
September 1984	Golf II	Diesel/ electric powered	Northwest of Oki Island	Unknown
January 1986	Echo II	Nuclear powered	Sea of Japan	Unknown

These thirteen submarines may represent the pick of Soviet technology: most of them nuclear powered, many of them doubtless nuclear armed. Yet only a few gave any indication as to what happened when they went down. The April 1968 Golf class submarine, a vessel of 2,350 to 2,800 tons with three to five missile-firing tubes, was salvaged by the CIA and found to have suffered an internal explosion. Three other submarines, the Echo I, the Whiskey, and the Charlie class vessels, were salvaged and towed away by Soviet ships. The Victor I class lost in 1984 actually collided with a U.S. aircraft carrier, the *Kitty Hawk*, which it was apparently following. The Echo II class submarine lost in 1986 suffered a fire on board and was located and towed away by Soviet vessels. The huge Yankee class nuclear submarine is still on the sea bottom near Guam, perhaps with sixteen launching tubes of nuclear missiles.

One explanation for the number of Soviet underwater disasters in the area of the Dragon Triangle is the shifting floor of the ocean itself. Because of the constant volcanic activity around Japan, the depth of the ocean is constantly in flux. Depths represented on charts have been known to change considerably before new charts could be prepared.

Constant remapping of the ocean floor in the area shows enormous alterations, with differences in depth of up to 1,000 feet. In recent memory, the floor of the Bonin Trench rose 6,000 feet. Sea mounts disappear and new ones form. Shallow areas become deep and new islands rise from the depths. Volcanic activity is especially marked east of Tokyo Bay. All of this represents a danger to shipping, but a special hazard for submarines, which must contend with underwater currents that may suddenly change as a result of seismic activity.

Another theory for the submarine disasters is the presence of sudden downdrafts, watery counterparts to the wind shear which takes airplanes down thousands of feet in seconds. Special storm conditions might cause an eddy in ocean water, bringing up the much denser water of the ocean floor. If a submarine is on the top of such a rising dome, all the water around it is much less dense. Slipping off the rising bubble would inevitably cause the submersible to descend. And, since this upwelling would cause considerable agitation in the neighboring water, the submarine would be buffeted by huge, violent underwater waves, perhaps as high as 500 feet from trough to crest.

Bouncing up and down on waves of such size would send the craft toward the sea bottom much faster than it could discharge ballast. The end would come when the waves brought it to a depth greater than the craft's ability to resist ocean pressure. The water's weight would simply crush the

Giant oceangoing tankers, some over 200,000 tons like the
California Maru (top) and the *Bolivar*, have vanished within the
Triangle. *(Photos from the Author's Collection)*

Below: Laid-up bulk carrier *La Carlota*, another mystery ship of the Dragon's Triangle. *(Photo: Peter Myers)*

Foot: The *Banaluna* was abandoned by its crew. No one knows what turned it into a Triangle ghost ship. *(Photo: National Maritime Museum, Greenwich, London)*

The *Maasgusar* spontaneously burst into flames within the Dragon's Triangle, although it had a noncombustible cargo. Note the triangular-shaped waves buffeting it. *(Photo reproduced by permission of the Kyodo News Service)*

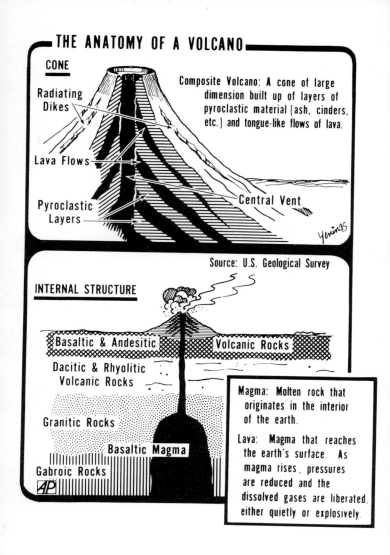

Composite drawing of a volcano. When a volcano erupts on the ocean floor, the released gases create awesome undersea turbulence. *(Illustration: Wide World)*

Right: The force of this underwater volcano 840 miles south of Tokyo was strong enough to create an island near Iwo Jima. Can you imagine its effect on craft sailing near it? *(Photo: Wide World)*

Below: A United States transport plane flying through the Dragon's Triangle saw this column of smoke rising from the sea. Photographer Ray Faxich reported the cloud to be four to five miles high. *(Photo: Wide World)*

Above: This eruption took place in 1986 – near Iwo Jima, one apex of the Dragon's Triangle. *(Photo: Wide World)*

Below: The Triangle's "Ring of Fire" at the bottom of the sea pushed a new island group from the ocean's floor in 1946. *(Photo: Wide World)*

Above: Ashes floating on the Pacific waters near undersea volcano Myojinsho. This eruption may have caused the disappearance of the *Kaio Maru No. 5* with thirty-one men aboard. Two islands appeared after the eruption but sank from sight as quickly.
(Photo: Wide World)

Below: Of the six hundred volcanoes active in the world today, the heaviest concentration lies within the Dragon's Triangle.
(Photo: Wide World)

Left: Sulfurous fumes
blot out the sun in
this spectacular –
and deadly –
volcanic display.
(Photo: Wide World)

Below: Magma, or
molten rock, hardens
on reaching the
cooler ocean surface
off the coast of Japan.
(Photo: Wide World)

vessel. Oceanographers came up with this theory to explain the disappearance of the USS *Thresher*, an atomic submarine which disappeared in the Atlantic depths on April 10, 1963. Even the most modern technological accomplishments of the superpowers must give way to the awesome might of the sea.

The fact that so many probably nuclear-armed Soviet submarines operate so close to Japan is naturally a cause for concern among the Japanese. But the USSR is not the only nuclear power posing an indirect threat to that nation.

Japan, understandably disturbed about the presence of unexploded atomic bombs in the ocean off her coasts, was considerably aroused by an incident which took place on December 6 or 7, 1965.

During U.S. maneuvers, an A-4E Skyhawk strike aircraft, equipped with a hydrogen bomb, somehow rolled off the flight deck of the United States aircraft carrier *Ticonderoga*. The plane and bomb have lain deep in the water ever since, with all the possibilities of an international espionage thriller. Apparently it has not yet been found, nor, as far as anyone knows, has it washed up on the many beaches or reefs of the islands of Japan. According to U.S. navy records the plane was lost on December 6, 1965, but apparently was not reported for twenty-four hours to avoid causing concern in Japan. In fact, since 1967, Japan has adopted a policy which has been called the "three nonnuclear principles." These are:

1. Prohibiting production of nuclear weapons by Japan
2. Prohibiting the possession of nuclear weapons by Japan
3. Prohibiting other nations from importing nuclear weapons into Japan

In a later investigation, a spokesman for the U.S. navy informed the Congress of the United States that the hydrogen bomb had disappeared at a distance of 500 miles from Japan, well outside Japan's territorial limits. But documents which were later declassified have since indicated that the bomb-bearing plane fell into the sea near Okinawa, still outside Japan's territorial limits but uncomfortably close to the home islands, where the people have long memories of destruction by atomic bombs. The missing bomb has not yet been found. It is calculated that bomb and plane are resting on the ocean floor at a depth of 16,000 feet, as presumably are the bombs and reactors that sank with the Soviet submarines.

Although salvage operations may have succeeded in bringing some of the nuclear warheads to the surface, the fact still remains that the waters around Japan—the legendary playground of that country's dragons—now boast an underwater nuclear arsenal of considerable proportions.

6

The Perseverance of Legend

The foundation of the Japanese islands is traditionally fixed at 2,300 years ago in legends connected with the sea. The legends are incorporated in ancient and sacred documents, the *Kojiki* and the *Nihongi* (or *Nihonshoki*), which tell of the beginnings of Japan and describe the long duration of the Imperial House from very ancient times to today.

In much of the world, calculation of historic events is based on a common pattern: B.C. and A.D. Japanese events are specified by the years of individual reigns of the long line of Japanese emperors from approximately 660 B.C. to 1989, all of the same dynasty.

The first emperor was Jimmu Tenno, the grandson of Ameraterasu-oho-mi-kami, Goddess of the Sun. The reign of each of his imperial successors was given a name. Each emperor begins a new era so that an event located by the year within the emperor's era is known not by the name of the emperor but by the name given to the years covered by his rule. This tradition of dating, and its historical solidity, has given a unity to the Japanese outlook on the world unmatched by that of other nations since Roman times, when the Romans calculated their events "since the founding of the city" (Rome)—*Ab urbe condita*.

Arab countries frequently follow a system of chronology dating from the year of the Hejira, when Mohammed fled Mecca and established a militant Islam. The western world follows the birth of Christ, although there is a tendency in scientific circles to replace B.C. and A.D. with B.C.E. (before the common era) and C.E. (common era). The Japanese alone, in conserving their imperial count for dates, have preserved tradition and a unified outlook into our own era, an era in which they are also among the leading modernists.

A non-Japanese person who reads a Japanese newspaper must interpolate the Western year of the emperor's ascension to the throne in order to know the Western date. For example, the Crown Prince Hirohito ascended to the throne in 1925, beginning the era of Showa (Eternal Peace). Thus, to find the Western date of any historical event in Hirohito's reign, one must add the number 1925 to the Showa date, since for Hirohito 1925 was Year One.

The Showa era ended with Emperor Hirohito's death in 1989, and a new era, the Heisei (Expanding Peace), began. Therefore 1990 is Heisei 2, and so on. This makes for a considerable amount of calculation for non-Japanese, but is indicative of the force of traditional memory and the cohesiveness of the Japanese spirit—having as they do their own system of year calculation, their own gods, and their own traditional account of how the Japanese islands rose out of the ocean.

Japanese mythology, as recounted in Shinto legends, does not concern itself with any other lands, or even the stars and the sky, but starts with the actions of the gods and the formation of the Japanese islands. This insular creation traditionally took place only several thousands of years ago. Japanese legends are therefore exclusively concerned with the islands of Japan, their creation by the gods, and the deeds of first mortals, Isonagi and Isonami, male and female.

The time span for the creation of Japan actually comes closer to geologic correctness than myths of other cultures making the creation of the earth, stars, and universe coeval. Evidence concerning the formation of the Japanese home islands indicates that this event took place in comparatively recent prehistoric times, in a series of oceanic convulsions in the Western Pacific close to the greatest depths in the world ocean, which covers more than 71 percent of the earth's surface.

It is in the area of Japan that islands have been observed to appear and to disappear, where submarine and surface volcanoes are still especially active in the Ring of Fire—the volcanic zone that circles the Pacific Ocean, where great whirlpools and sudden giant waves tear apart fishing boats and huge cargo ships alike. It is also in this area that recorded earthquakes have attained the almost unbelievable frequency of 21,000 for the months of June and July 1989.

It may be possible that the Japanese came to their islands in a comparatively recent era, as indicated by the traditions of the line of emperors starting with the Emperor Jimmu Tenno in 660 B.C. According to some theories, the original Japanese colonists came to Japan from other islands in the Pacific—islands which now lie below the surface of the ocean—at the time of a great cataclysmic rectification of land and sea areas. Examination of the Pacific floor indicates, as in other parts of the world, that large contiguous areas of the ocean floor were once land and that other parts of the sea bottom have risen. This may explain the recurring legends of lost land masses in the Pacific, as some of the Pacific island chains are merely the upper reaches of great mountains now sunk beneath the sea.

This antique and inbred memory of the sea, reinforced by Japan's position in the ocean, literally balanced on the edge of the Pacific drop-off into the Ogasawara and other deeps to the south. Though considered in former times to be a literally bottomless gulf, it has not altered Japan's use of the ocean, nor the courage of her fishermen and seamen in navigating it.

Tales from Japan's medieval times tell of the sea's dangers, with legends of vanished fleets, great dragons and other monsters whose activities cause whirlpools and tidal waves, and destructive seaquakes that swallow ships and islands. But at the same time there have occurred what seems to be beneficent intervention on the part of the gods, raising great winds and seas against enemy invaders of Japan.

This happened twice in the thirteenth century when the *kami-kaze* (or "divine wind") scattered and sank the ships of invading Mongol armies from China and Korea, and inspired the Japanese to defeat and massacre those who had been able to land.

In 1274 Kublai Khan, Emperor of China and grandson of Genghis Khan, the Mongol conqueror who shook the world, sent an army composed, among other units, of the disciplined cavalry hordes who had conquered most of Asia, Russia, and Europe as far as Hungary. This huge army, secure in its overwhelming numbers, training, medieval artillery, and terror-inspiring reputation, landed at Hakozaki Bay. In the ensuing battle, the Japanese held firm along the east coast of Kyushu, while the Mongols regrouped. Suddenly a tremendous typhoon struck, sinking hundreds of the invaders' ships and blowing others back to the coast of Korea.

Six years later the Mongols tried again, with an even larger army and more ships. On this occasion they were able to land in great force and the battle lasted for almost two months, with the Japanese still holding the invaders along the coast of Kyushu. But the *kami-kaze* again roared out of the sky, wrecking and sinking the ships of two Mongol fleets, and drowning their crews. Those Mongols still alive on the flooded battlefield never made it back to China and Kublai Khan, who understandably did not make a third attempt to conquer Japan.

Prior to help from the *kami-kaze*, Japanese forces had previously received legendary miraculous help from the sea in the third century. Queen Jingu, widow of an emperor, was helped by underwater denizens. While Jingu with her fleet was on her way to conquer Korea, a tremendous storm occurred in the North China Sea, putting the fleet in great peril. But the sudden appearance of large banks of huge fish billowing up against the ships' sides kept them afloat, allowing them to survive the storm and proceed with the conquest.

Even more striking is the legend of the *Heike gani*, or the "crabs of Heike." According to historic accounts, a naval battle was fought in medieval times between the powerful Heike and Minamoto clans, a battle which the Heike lost. The dead Heike warriors, while floating down to the sea bottom, assumed the shape of crabs, and the descendants of these crabs still show, on their shells, the faces, helmets, and accoutrements of the drowned combatants.

This last is not a legend, as the backs of the crabs show an extraordinary likeness to the faces of ancient warriors as illustrated in medieval Japanese prints. Most of the animals show only what looks like the face of a one-time combatant, but the larger crabs, called *taishogani* ("colonel crabs") or *tatsugashira* ("dragon helmet crabs"), are supposed to be the ghost pictures of the Heike officers. These officer crabs bear on their shells not only a face, but helmets with horns, sometimes with what appears to be a dragon insignia, and other features common to the visors and helmets worn in medieval times by the officers of Japan's feudal armies.

Like the legend of the *kami-kaze*, which cannot really be classified as a legend because the decisive events did occur, the crabs of Heike possess an element of incredible coincidence, inasmuch as anyone who buys one can contemplate, before eating it, the fierce, angry, and resolute features of a long-dead samurai.

However, the most enduring myths of the sea in the Far East, both in China and Japan, deal with those mysterious creatures known as dragons.

The Eastern dragon should not be confused with its Western counterpart. Whereas the Western dragon is generally associated with evil and destruction, or greedily maintaining a treasure hoard, the Eastern dragon is generally presented as a benevolent creature, if somewhat capricious.

According to Chinese mythology, the dragon, or *lung*, controlled storms and was often associated with water spirits. Storms resulted when dragons were angry. According to a Chinese author of the third century B.C., dragons could rarely be seen by mankind—but their actions could, as when they rose to the sky assisted by wind and rain. Other authors associated dragons with whirlwinds that carry heavy objects into the sky. At sea, cyclonic waterspouts were interpreted as dragons winging their way to the upper air. Volcanoes, too, were connected with dragons—these were the holes from which they commenced their flights.

The most powerful of dragons acted as the kings of the four seas located at the cardinal points of the Chinese compass. The sea king of the Western Sea (the Pacific) was the Li-Lung, who lived in a great undersea palace filled with riches from the cargoes of wrecked junks.

Then there was the legend of the underwater dragon palace five or six days' sailing from the city of Suzhou, with its always turbulent water, strange sounds, daily submergence, and the eerie red light, as bright as the sun, which hung over the location by night. Perhaps the Chinese seamen were trying to describe an underwater volcano off the coast of Japan. The red light that rises from beneath the sea could, for instance, be connected with the phenomenon we now call the UFO.

An interesting note is offered by the twelve animals of the Chinese zodiac, a calendar form dating back to 2600 B.C. The Chinese years are the Rat, the Ox, the Tiger, the Rabbit, the Dragon, the Serpent, the Horse, the Sheep, the Monkey, the Cock, the Dog, and the Pig. Of all of these, the dragon is the only creature which cannot be encountered in the flesh—at least nowadays. Dr. N. B. Dennys, a leading early expert on Chinese mythology, expressed the opinion that there was "little doubt" that China had once been the home of actual dragons.

Dragon bones and teeth were considered sovereign remedies in the Chinese pharmacopoeia, responsible for curing such conditions as dysentery, gallstones, infantile fever and convulsions, internal infections and ulcers, paralysis of the legs, illnesses of pregnant women, and remittent fever and abscesses. Blowing powdered bones into the nose or ears stopped bleeding, and also cured navel abscesses on babies.

Preparing these bones—which may have been fossils of the great lizards and mammals of prehistoric times—required much work. Bones had to be boiled with certain herbs, or roasted over a fire until red-hot, then ground into powder. They could not come into contact with iron or fish. In any event, the raw materials for such medicines were offered for sale in the apothecary stalls of such cities as Hong Kong and Peking. In fact, Western paleontologists could often be found browsing the dragon bone bins of these stores, for some of these remedies were actually ancient fossils. The teeth that led to the discovery of Peking Man were "unearthed" in this manner.

Certainly, Chinese belief in dragons has extended into the twentieth century, as a report in the 1932 book *A Dictionary of Chinese Mythology* by E. T. C. Warner shows. In May of 1931, in the predominantly communist province of Kiangsi, a dragon was seen on the Kan River, supposedly responsible for a major flood in the area. Warner writes:

> As the Book of History recorded that some 2,000 years ago the people used to offer the fairest maiden every year to the Ho Po, the God of the River, to be his concubine, it is now suggested that some suitable sacrifice should be presented to the dragon. It is said that if his wrath is appeased, the flood will subside. On the other hand, if nothing is done to please the creature, it would make the Kiangsi people suffer more besides the flood and the communist uprisings.

There is, however, no record as to whether or not the dragon received a human sacrifice as a result of this suggestion.

In Japan the dragon is called *Tatsu* or *Ryu*, and was seen as a sea god, and also as a river god—a river god to whom, some evidence indicates, human sacrifices occasionally were made. A strange association with these divine dragons is the mysterious lights in the sky, which often move from the woods to the sea. There is one story of a light which arises from the sea and then flies to one of the mountains, where it hangs in an old pine tree outside a Buddhist temple. This is called the Dragon Lantern, and is supposedly an offering sent by the dragons of the sea to the shrine's deities.

Okakoro-Kakuzo in his *Book of Tea* writes of the dragon in this way:

The dragon is the spirit of change. . . . Coiled in the unfathomed depths of the sea. . . . He unfolds himself in the stormcloud, he washes his mane in the darkness of the seething whirlpools. His claws are the fork of the lightning. . . . His voice is heard in the hurricanes. . . . The dragon reveals himself only to vanish.

This description is remarkably similar to one printed in 1901 in the Japanese nature magazine *Shizen Shimbun*, which told of a gigantic sea creature. This creature was seen only on stormy nights, and by flashes of lightning.

The steamer *Chillagoe*, commanded by Captain W. Firth, made a sighting of a creature in 1902. It was described as being thirty-five feet long, with four very large fins, and having a seal's head of gigantic proportions. The ship came very close before this monster submerged.

Similar sightings took place in the Indian Ocean, with a passenger on the Dutch steamer *Java* catching sight of the head of a sea serpent rising approximately six feet out of the water in 1906, and a sighting from the steamer *Zondel* described a similar creature the following year.

Sea monsters were sighted south of Japan by the ship *Nestor* heading for Shanghai in 1976, and by the ship *Georgia* out of Rangoon in 1977.

On the other side of the Pacific in 1970, the freight-passenger ship *President Grant*, en route to Los Angeles, encountered mysterious trouble—strange vibrations at the bow, with a radically different wake. Examination showed that the 14,000 ton ship had impaled a giant sea beast on its bow. The remains were never identified, merely being described as a large marine animal of uncertain species.

And in the Atlantic, in 1947, a similar report was radioed from the Grace Lines passenger ship *Santa Clara*—that it had struck a forty-five foot creature. The three witnesses to the incident were the chief mate, Mr. William Humphreys, the third officer, Mr. John Axelson, and the navigation officer, Mr. John Rigney. When interviewed, Axelson said that he had noticed the creature's head appear abruptly from beneath the water: "It was noticed that the water was stained red. . . . It was believed, because of the color of the water, that the sea monster had been hit by the keel of our ship. This assumption even now seems valid, as the animal twisted and thrashed in a manner suggesting it was severely hurt . . ."

In these more recent cases, we see a modern reversal of the tales of ancient and medieval times, when small fishing craft attacked by sea monsters were often demolished. Nowadays, motorized ships sometimes run over and destroy monsters that in earlier days would have destroyed *them*. But even in modern times the number of disappearances of ships with modern equipment and means of communication in the area of the Dragon Triangle has resurrected a certain memory of regional tales and old legends, even tales of sea monsters, some of which resemble dragons.

However alien this may be to the concepts of modern geology and paleontology, not to mention the assurance of science that sea monsters and sea serpents have not existed since Jurassic times, Japanese fishing boats sometimes encounter creatures at sea which seem to resemble these fabled monsters.

One such incident occurred in the southern part of the Dragon Triangle in 1977, when the captain of a fishing boat, appropriately named the *Sea Dragon*, captured a sea monster and then, after photographing it, tried to keep it on board with the intention of bringing it back to Japan for study. However, when the two-ton specimen began to decompose he had it thrown over the side without even trying to keep the skeleton, which would certainly have been more valuable than his total catch. For, according to examination of the photograph, what he had thrown away was the carcass of a plesiosaur, a creature supposedly extinct for sixty million years.

If the captain had kept his "dragon" or plesiosaur, it would not have been the only living fossil known to science. Only fifty years ago, the world of science was confronted with the first clue that creatures presumed to be long extinct still lived in the deep waters of the oceans.

On December 22, 1938, fishermen netted a large, odd-looking fish in the waters off South Africa. It was dark blue, four and a half feet long, and weighed 127 pounds, with heavy scales and large, bulging, deep blue eyes. This strange catch survived for some time on the trawler's deck, snapping viciously at any who came near.

The creature died before the trawler made port, and the decomposing body was taken to the local museum in New London, South Africa. The curator, Marjory Courtenay-Latimer, sent a sketch of the creature to Dr. J. L. B. Smith, professor of ichthyology at Rhodes University. As the letter was delayed by Christmas mail, thus preventing a response, the curator finally had the specimen skinned and mounted. The only other sample saved from the now putrid remains was the fish's skull.

Smith recognized the creature immediately as a coelacanth, a fish with lobe fins that looked like legs. The species was well known to paleontologists—supposedly it had become extinct at the end of the Cretaceous period, sixty million years ago.

Smith named the creature *chalumnae Latimeria,* and told the world that it now had a living coelacanth. It caused a storm of popular interest, and also a good amount of scientific argument. Up to that time, all specimens of the extinct coelacanth were small. Most measured five inches, while the largest measured twenty inches. As it turned out, these samples were of marsh-dwelling species. Only after World War II were the fossil remains of a five-foot coelacanth discovered, in Germany.

Dr. Smith offered a reward for another specimen, which was not claimed until after World War II. In 1952, a fisherman in the Comoro Islands off Mozambique caught a strange fish and showed it to a local teacher, who remembered the reward—three years' income for the islanders. Word was sent to Smith, this time, just before the Christmas holidays. Since this date, additional specimens have turned up, including a female bearing eggs. Live coelacanths have even been photographed underwater.

The fish is not unknown to fisherfolk of the Indian Ocean. There, the coelacanth is known as the *kombessa*—an edible, but not very prized, catch.

Still more interesting is a story from Tampa, Florida, where, in 1949, a woman ran a small shop making tourist souvenirs, mainly out of fish scales purchased from local fishermen. One such fisher sold her a gallon can full of large fish scales, tarpon-size (about the size of a silver dollar). They were not, however, tarpon scales. Curious, the souvenir maker sent one to the National Museum in Washington, where the specimen was sent to Dr. Isaac Ginsburg of the Department of Fishes.

Dr. Ginsburg had never seen such a scale before—to the best of his knowledge no fish with such scales lived in American waters. He appeared to have the scale of an ancient fish, possibly a coelacanth. He wrote to Tampa immediately, asking for more information, but never received a reply. Perhaps all the other scales were sold, and now gather dust as ancient reminders of happy vacations. But this single scale would seem to indicate that an ancient fish, perhaps the coelacanth, lives in the waters off Florida—perhaps in the depths of the area known as the Bermuda Triangle.

Perhaps the plesiosaur and the coelacanth, as well as other

living fossils, were shielded from the theoretical Cosmic Ray Extinction of Cretaceous times by living in or adapting to the ocean depths. The prehistoric reptile or animal captured by the *Sea Dragon* is one more manifestation of the surprises that may be expected in the Dragon Triangle.

Plesiosaurs have also been placed in the triangles of mystery by scientific sources. In 1969, the DSRV (Deep Submergence Research Vessel) *Alvin* was following telephone cables in the deeps of the Tongue of the Ocean near the Bahamas, an area encompassed in the Bermuda Triangle. Captain McCamis looked up from the control board to see a shadowy figure swimming away from the *Alvin*—a figure that looked remarkably like the extinct plesiosaur.

For centuries before science knew the conformations of prehistoric animals, sailors described sea monsters which resembled the plesiosaur. In the catacombs of Rome, a sculptured coffin offers a view of Jonah being swallowed, not by a whale, but by a creature which looks amazingly like the plesiosaur. The creature has a long, thin neck, relatively small head, heavy body, thick but tapering tail, and four powerful flippers. From paleontological records, plesiosaurs attained a length of up to forty-five feet.

Ivan Sanderson reported a case from 1969 which took place in the northern Pacific when an Alaskan shrimper picked up what appeared to be a distinctly plesiosaur-shaped reading on its echo sounder. This location is significant, for fifty-three sightings of sea monsters have been recorded between Alaska and Oregon from 1812 to the present.

This sonar sighting took place while the ship was dragging for shrimp off Raspberry Island near Kodiak in the Shelikof Strait. The specimen traced, however, could have extended up to 150 feet—a "dragon" large enough to strike fear even into the hearts of modern skippers.

The plesiosaur is also offered as the solution to another enigma of natural science: the Loch Ness Monster.

Besides the creatures sighted in Loch Ness and Loch Alst, and the other lochs with their water horses, several lakes in Ireland are reputed to be the haunts of large creatures, and there are similar traditions for lakes in Sweden, Norway, and Iceland. Our own country has had well-documented sightings of large creatures in California, Minnesota, Montana, Nevada, Oregon, Utah, Wisconsin, Alaska, and in Lake Champlain between New York and Vermont. Canada also boasts lake creatures in British Columbia, Manitoba, Quebec, and Ontario, with some even near large cities like Toronto.

Theorists have gone so far as to propose a "lake monster zone" at roughly latitude 60 degrees in the Northern Hemisphere. Recent reports from the USSR and China may suggest that the theorists have a point, with the existence of so-called lake monsters in those countries as well.

Although no one believes in dragons anymore, except possibly emotionally, the form of a truly great dragon can be traced on a map familiar to all. The map is that of Japan, whose seven islands, closely connected, form a recognizable image of a giant dragon. Its horns, head, and mouth is the northern island of Hokkaido. Its neck goes down close to its body at Hakodate. Its body and the shape of some of its claws is the island of Honshu, west of Kyushu. Its lower extremities and tail begin with Kyushu. South of Kyushu, its tail appears all the way south to Okinawa.

In past times earthquakes were often attributed to a great dragon living in caverns underneath the sea who frequently changed its position as it slept. When we consider that the recorded earthquakes in Japan, in a period of little more than one month, reached the staggering number of 21,000, we conclude that, although terrifying to foreign visitors, many of these earth tremors are scarcely noticed by a people almost inured for centuries to the shakings of the earth. These earthquakes are now understood, yet are no more possible to control, than the legendary stirrings of the subterranean dragon sleeping under the islands of Japan.

7

Ghost Ships of the Dragon Triangle

Legends from past centuries concerning the Dragon Triangle have continued down to the present. Sometimes they suggest explanations to what seem to be paranormal occurrences, and sometimes, despite the corroboration of witnesses, these occurrences are as mysterious as the legends of earlier days.

An incident reminiscent of the *Flying Dutchman* legend occurred north of the Ogasawara island chain in January 1989 when a whaling ship encountered and almost collided with a ketch that was sailing erratically on the whaler's course. There seemed to be someone at the wheel, but when Captain Morio Sakagami and several others climbed aboard the ketch they made a grisly discovery. They found that the helmsman was a partially decomposed corpse, half standing and loosely fastened to the wheel. He appeared to have been dead for several weeks prior to the time that the crew members of the whaler came aboard. No other members of the dead man's crew were found, although the ketch should have had a crew of four or five.

The dead man apparently died from a wound inflicted by the cutlass which was still sticking between his ribs. The scabbard of the cutlass lay on the deck. A single word was written on it in blood—the word "depths." On the cutlass itself a name had been etched—Bully Bates—but there was no indication whether this name was that of the victim or the murderer. Captain Sakagami turned the matter over to the Japanese police, who, lacking witnesses, suspects, or motives, have not come up with the answer.

The story of the *Flying Dutchman* has become so famous in seafaring legends that all ghost ships that move under sail (even when there is no wind) are associated with her. Although originally an apparition identified with the Cape of Good Hope and the passage to the Indies, this ghost ship of other days has allegedly been seen by many seamen and the legend is credited by many others. The *Flying Dutchman* is a seventeenth-century ship whose captain cursed God in his struggle to round Cape Horn in 1680, swearing that he would continue to try until Judgment Day. In punishment, the captain and his crew were doomed to continue their voyage, eternally trying—and failing—to round the Horn. Certainly, the ship never reached its destination of Batavia. But other ships have reported seeing a ghost ship in the area. Usually when such a sighting is made, one of the crew members of the sighting ship dies soon afterward, falling from the rigging or into the sea.

The *Flying Dutchman* was encountered by a British warship on the night of June 11, 1881. A naval ensign on watch duty aboard the HMS *Inconstant* sailing southeast of Japan made the following notation in the ship's log, describing an incident which had also been witnessed by at least a dozen other crew members:

> At 4:00 A.M. "The Flying Dutchman" crossed our bows. She emitted a strange phosphorescent light as of a phantom ship all aglow, in the midst of which light the masts, spars, and sails of a brig 200 yards distant stood out in strong relief as she came up on the port bow where also the officer of the watch from the bridge saw her, as did also the quarterdeck midshipman, who was sent forward at once to the forecastle, but on arriving there was no vestige nor any sign whatever of any material ship to be seen either near or right away to the horizon, the night being clear and the sea calm.

The naval ensign's rather nonchalant report of a ghost ship and his immediate identification of it as the *Flying Dutchman* went apparently unquestioned by the captain of the British warship, possibly because the ensign was an English prince, later to become King George V of England.

Visions shared by many seamen on the oceans of the world by night or by day of old sailing vessels in full sail may, of course, be induced by a collective belief in legends of the past. Once the legend, especially such a vivid one as the *Flying Dutchman*, becomes established in the consciousness of seafarers, it becomes relatively easy to convince oneself and others that the shape of the legendary ship has come into view. Especially so if, after such a sighting, a seaman is killed in an accident or disappears for some other reason, such as falling into the sea.

A single ghost, allegedly encountered by a number of seamen in the Western Pacific, is the Chinless Officer, a ship's officer, a second mate, who appears during the night watch on the bridge of a merchant ship, checks the course, and asks about radio weather information. At first it is presumed by crew members that he is the duty officer on watch. Most of his lower face is covered by a muffler. Sometimes the muffler drops and he leaves or disappears without further conversation, leaving the helmsman in a state of shock after seeing that the officer is not the second officer on board but a person or apparition whose lower face has been torn off. This incident is usually followed by some disaster to the ship's personnel or to the ship itself.

The ghostly Chinless Officer must have actually existed within fairly recent times. Mariner's folklore has it that his missing jaw was removed by a sweeping hook at the end of a crane as it swung from its position near one of the hatches to a lighter alongside. He died as a result of shock and lack of adequate medical attention. Since then he has become a frequently reported psychic phenomenon among merchant mariners.

An earlier reported ghost along the Pacific seaways was the famous "Ladylips," allegedly the captain of the *Ville de Paris*, a French gunboat, in 1782. In order to evade the pursuing British, the gunboat sailed around the tip of South America into the Pacific and was blown westward. When supplies gave out, the men tried to fish with *flannel* on a boat hook; a shark, snagged on the line, hit "Ladylips" with the boat hook, tearing away his jaw. As he lay bleeding, he slashed his wrists to hasten an end to his suffering, offering the blood to his men, who eventually reached a Pacific island after finishing off the captain. "Ladylips" has been seen by crews of merchant and war vessels. In all, more than five hundred persons have said that they have seen him standing over the sea or among the yards—as reported by Vincent Gaddis, "in places where it would be impossible for a living man to be."

Ghost ships—phantoms or real ships that have disappeared— are reputed still to sail the seas and sometimes cause other ships to share their fate and sink. This type of legend, however fantastic, may be the simple truth, considering the following possibility.

A number of ships which have disappeared in the Dragon Triangle have been sunk by USOs—the term applied to Unidentified Submarine Objects. It has been noted both in the Atlantic and Pacific oceans that a number of ship sinkings have been caused by collision with hulks of other ships which have already sunk. These hulks, for a variety of reasons, do not rest on the sea bottom but float relatively near the surface. They follow the prevailing currents and are further propelled by surface storms and undersea seismic movements. As mentioned before, such hulks are considered extreme navigation hazards and every effort is made to chart their locations so that maritime authorities such as the coast guard can destroy them.

Perhaps the floating hulk theory may also serve to explain the disappearances of some submarines, whose maps might show the location of known wrecks, but not the moving ones.

Some ships disappear, reappear, and then are lost again, a phenomenon that has repeated itself on all the oceans. There are many stories of ships finding derelicts, putting prize crews aboard, and then losing both derelict and crew. Some ghost ships sail on for a period after they are abandoned by their crews. One celebrated example is the case of the French steamer *Frigorifique*, which was struck by the coal ship *Rumney* in a fog and abandoned by her crew when she began taking on water. Crew and passengers were celebrating their rescue aboard the *Rumney* when the *Frigorifique* hove into view out of the fog, narrowly missing the coal ship. The *Frigorifique* appeared once again, this time ramming the *Rumney*. Survivors from the French vessel and the English crew both had to take to the lifeboats again.

Sometimes, ships that are known to have sunk float again to the surface because of trapped air pockets or the loss of heavy cargo. A strange incident took place with the *Dahama*, a ship which sank with a heavy cargo of sugar. When the sugar melted in the water, the *Dahama* floated to the surface.

Occasionally there is no credible explanation for a particular missing ship. In 1967 Tokyo Marine Radio received a signal from the *Cleveland*, a tanker of 10,265 tons belonging to the Cleveland Transport Company of New York. The message stated that there was an engine room fire, which the crew was fighting. A subsequent message was then received reporting that the ship was taking on water and that the crew was abandoning ship.

An air-sea search was at once initiated and an oil slick discovered off Sasebo, which would coincide with the approximate area given as the *Cleveland*'s position. When no further indications were found the search was called off and the Japanese Maritime Safety Agency duly advised the Cleveland Transport Company of the sinking of their ship.

To the surprise of the agency's representatives, the Cleveland Transport Company denied the loss, replying that the *Cleveland* was in Bombay, a considerable distance from Japan. But when the Bombay anchorage was checked, it was found that the ship was no longer there.

How had she made a distress call close to Sasebo? According to the date she cleared port in Bombay it would have been impossible for her to be near enough to Sasebo to enable her to make a distress call from the vicinity unless she were capable of a surface speed of at least 120 knots, or 140 miles per hour in landsmen's terms. The top speed of a tanker is less than one-sixth this incredible speed. Neither the answer to this question nor the ship herself was ever found, nor was the mystery of how she so speedily sailed (or was teleported?) close to Japan ever clarified.

Another mystery within a mystery occurred aboard *La Carlota*, a Philippines flagship formerly the *Salvador II* and renamed in 1977. In 1987, while the ship was sailing in the Dragon Triangle, a spontaneous fire broke out. There were no combustible materials near or in the chain locker section where the fire first occurred. And despite efforts by the crew to extinguish it, it kept burning. As they fought it in one section of the ship, a new fire would start to blaze in a different section. Although the crew could not extinguish them, the fires suddenly abated by themselves.

The fire-damaged *Carlota* is still anchored in Manila, but cannot be sold or demolished until the authorities ascertain what actually happened at sea in the strange case of the self-igniting fire.

A mystery rivaling that of the *Marie Celeste* can also be found in the Pacific, in the strange case of the ship *Joyita*. Built in 1931 as a luxury yacht, this seventy ton, sixty-nine foot vessel became the prototypical hard-luck ship. Her original owner was a Hollywood director, but the film connection was severed after the star Thelma Todd died mysteriously aboard. The *Joyita* was requisitioned as a patrol boat during World War II, only to run aground in Hawaii. Most of her lower hull had to be replanked. After the war, the ship was converted to a fishing boat, with her interior gutted to install refrigerated holds. Six hundred twenty cubic feet of cork was inserted for insulation.

The ship was finally chartered in 1953 to a British seaman, Lieutenant Commander Thomas Henry "Dusty" Miller. His fishing business was not a success, and by 1955, Miller was in Samoa—and in deep financial trouble. It was at this point that he met R. D. Pearless, the newly appointed district officer to the Tokelau Islands 270 miles to the north. Pearless wanted to establish better communications for his islands, and attempted to arrange a yearly charter of the *Joyita*. When this plan failed, he negotiated a charter for the boat through a copra shipping firm.

The windfall could not have come at a better time. At this point, Miller had been reduced to living alone on the ship, unable to finance any more fishing trips, pay his crew, or even buy food for himself.

At 11:00 A.M. on October 2, 1955, the *Joyita* prepared to sail from Apia, Samoa. She carried a considerable cargo of foodstuffs and medical supplies desperately needed in the Tokelaus. Pearless was aboard, along with Dr. A. D. Parsons of the Apia hospital, a pharmacist, and seven Tokelau islanders who had been stranded on Samoa. In addition, sixteen crewmen were aboard, as well as two representatives from the copra company.

They soon found that the ship was badly maintained. Even before the *Joyita* managed to leave port, a puff of smoke burst from the ship's side and it began to drift. One of the ship's engines had failed. Miller assured port officials that it would be easily fixed after a few hours. The *Joyita* did not leave until midnight, and even then, it was operating with only one engine, for the clutch on the port engine had been disconnected.

At the ship's destination, the port of Fakaofu, the Tokelau islanders eagerly awaited the *Joyita*'s arrival. But as time passed and the ship did not appear, they became worried. Finally the ship was reported overdue, and a search was initiated on October 6. For the better part of the following week, nearly 100,000 square miles were swept with no trace of the ship.

The search had been terminated for nearly a month when on November 10 the supply ship *Tuvalu* radioed the Fiji Islands that she had spotted the *Joyita*, some 450 miles west-southwest of Samoa. The ship was listing heavily, with much of the deck underwater. A steering position atop the deckhouse had been smashed, and a canvas awning had been rigged. None of the twenty-five people who had set off in the ship were aboard, nor was the log or any message found.

Immediately, the mystery began to deepen. It almost seemed as if the *Joyita* had been following a course directly opposite the one she should have taken, and it was found that large amounts of food and enough fuel for a 3,000 mile voyage had been taken aboard at Apia. Examination of the ship revealed that the remaining engine had failed, with repairs attempted on the other. No useful navigational instruments remained on the ship, and the outboard-powered dinghy, along with ten- and sixteen-person life rafts, were missing. A renewed search was made in the area, but the boat, the rafts, and the people were never found.

The *Joyita*'s hull had sustained minor damage from wave action, but seemed seaworthy. The cause of the flooding was a corroded seawater coolant pipe below the engine room floorboards. Further examination uncovered the reason no SOS had been received, although there was evidence that one had been transmitted. The lead to the radio aerial had a break eighteen inches above the transmitter, giving the radio a working range of only about two miles.

The mystery of why the derelict vessel had not been spotted by searchers was partially answered during the towing operation into Suva in the Fijis. The metal towing vessel, the *Degei*, showed clearly on radar screens twenty miles away. The wooden *Joyita* projected no image, even when radar was close.

Investigation at the port revealed that besides the crew, the ship's cargo had disappeared. Also a waterlogged doctor's bag was found, with a corroded stethoscope, a scalpel, some needles and catgut, and several bloodstained bandages.

Theories from sea monsters to pirates were aired in the local press. The *Joyita*'s course would have intersected the operations of a Japanese fishing fleet, and the enemies from the still-recent war were held up as possible villains. Perhaps District Officer Pearless had seen something he was not supposed to see.

Twenty-eight witnesses were called for a court of inquiry, which on February 22, 1956, issued its findings. Describing the disaster to the ship was easy enough. The leak under the engines had caused flooding throughout the ship, especially since the bilge pumps did not work. Because the engine was flooded, the ship was left helpless in the sea. But the commissioners were baffled as to what happened to the passengers and crew. It seemed as if the dinghy and rafts had been removed, and there was a remote possibility that survivors might be on any of the hundreds of small islands in the area. Much blame was laid on Miller for taking an unsafe vessel to sea without a working radio or a well-stocked lifeboat. Perhaps the only reason he had taken the risk was because of the cork insulation in the hold. As Miller told one port official at Apia, "If anything did happen to this boat a man would be a fool to leave her because she's unsinkable."

The *Joyita* was auctioned off, overhauled, and back at sea in 1956. But she went aground in 1957 with thirteen passengers aboard, then again in 1959. With a reputation as a ghost and bad-luck ship, she was left as a hulk on the island of Levuka.

There the *Joyita* was bought by the author Robin Maugham, who developed his own theory on the tragedy: In the evening of October 3, the *Joyita* encountered rough weather which broke the corroded pipe in the bilge. The pumps didn't work, and when the engines were flooded, the ship lost steerage way, and became unmanageable. At 10:25, when the clock stopped, a wave smashed into the steering house, which was built of lightweight lumber, smashed away the port side, and began flooding the hold. This is when the ship was abandoned.

The medical equipment and bandages indicated that someone had required treatment. Maugham suggested that person was Miller. With the ship seemingly sinking and the only man who knew it to be unsinkable lying unconscious, it would be understandable for the passengers and part of the crew to swarm into the rafts. Perhaps some of the Europeans remained on board. One of the crewmen, Tanini, was devoted to Miller. When the first mate sighted a reef in the distance, and with a favorable wind, everyone got on the rafts. However, the ocean currents in the area took them in the opposite direction, to disappear.

Miller may have remained on the ship, guarded by Tanini, and protected by the canvas awning, which was tied with sailor's knots and attached to part of the wrecked wheelhouse. Maugham theorizes that Miller died, and the *Joyita* drifted on, with only Tanini alive. When Japanese fishermen intercepted the vessel, the islander, starved and not quite sane, attacked them, perhaps falling overboard in the struggle. Finding a boat seemingly on the point of sinking, the Japanese, who had come as rescuers, not as pirates, decided to take the cargo and then left the *Joyita* to sink—which it did not.

Maugham admitted that his theory is sheer guesswork. But without a survivor to tell the real story, the *Joyita* had already drifted far from fact and onto the seas of conjecture.

Students of the unusual can find an ample supply of true sea stories in the Pacific. Consider the last voyage of the *Melanesian*, a motorized vessel of 130 tons that set off from Sikiana Atoll on a routine interisland service trip. Sixty-four people were on board when the ship set off—they were never seen again. After reporting in near the island of Sikerane, the *Melanesian* seemed to disappear.

Subsequently, a piece of timber was found, along with a buoyancy tank—and the body of the ship's boatswain. The body and the tank had both been subjected to tremendous pressure. A court of inquiry debated whether the *Melanesian* had struck a mine, but finally came to the conclusion that the ship had been smashed by some enormous, unidentifiable force.

The yacht *Annette* was the mystery ship of 1958. It set off from the island of Apia to Suva in the Fijis, but was found sunk on Dibble's Reef, near the island of Vanua Levu. The ship's rigging was intact, but the hull had been holed by the coral reef. Everything aboard seemed in its proper place—except for the married couple who had set off in the ship. The *Annette*'s dinghy was missing, but this came ashore approximately sixty miles away. Although its outboard motor was missing, it carried a pair of oars and a water bottle, making it seem unlikely that the boat had overturned to drown its occupants.

One of the grimmer stories of the Pacific is that of the ketch *Wing On*. The ship was found in 1940 canted on a reef in the Fijis, with three sails rigged and the tiller lashed. The ship seemed deserted, but when investigators boarded her, they found a starving woman in the flooded ship's cabin, just barely keeping her head above the water. As the rescuers pulled her to safety, they discovered that she had been trying to hold up the body of another woman. Subsequent searching turned up the decomposed body of a man.

The group had originally comprised two young married couples attempting to sail from San Francisco to the Marquesa Islands. Their boat was leaky, with faulty pumps, and the navigational equipment was defective. Becoming lost, they ran out of food, and nearly starved to death while drifting 2,000 miles beyond their original destination.

The Pacific's mysteries are not limited to seagoing craft. Something terrifying happened in the air one day in the late summer of 1939—and to this day the incident is shrouded in secrecy.

All that is known is that a military transport plane left the Marine Naval Air Station in San Diego at 3:30 one afternoon. Three hours later, as the plane was over the Pacific Ocean, a frantic distress signal was sounded. Then the radio signal died.

A little later the plane limped back to base and made an emergency landing. Ground crew members rushed to the craft and when they boarded, they were horrified to see twelve dead men. The only survivor was the copilot, who, though badly injured, had stayed alive long enough to bring the plane back. A few minutes later he was dead, too.

All of the bodies had large, gaping wounds. Even weirder, the pilot and copilot had emptied their .45 Colt automatic pistols at something. The empty shells were found lying on the floor of the cockpit. A foul, sulfuric odor pervaded the interior of the craft.

The exterior of the airplane was badly damaged, looking as if it had been struck by missiles. The personnel who boarded the craft came down with an odd skin infection.

Strict security measures were quickly put into effect and the emergency ground crew was ordered to leave the plane. The job of removing the bodies and investigating the incident was left to three medical officers.

The incident was successfully hushed up and did not come to light for fifteen years, when investigator Robert Coe Gardner learned of it from someone who was there. The mystery of what the crew encountered in midair that afternoon in 1939 has never been solved.

Another aerial mystery caused a worldwide sensation in the 1930s, and it still stands as one of the world's great enigmas. When aviatrix Amelia Earhart vanished, along with her navigator, on the third-to-last leg of a round-the-world flight in 1937, she made the transition from celebrity to legend.

The third-to-last leg of her flight, to the refueling stop at Howland Island, was the most difficult of the entire journey. It involved a trip over 2,556 miles of open water to find an island two miles long and half a mile wide. At 10:30 A.M. on July 2, 1937, the Electra took off. The USS *Ontario* was stationed halfway between Lae and Howland to act as guard, with the USS *Swan* taking the same job between Howland and Hawaii. A U.S. Coast Guard cutter, the *Itasca*, was posted at Howland to send and receive radio homing signals.

The flight should have taken eighteen hours. Instead, the radio messages received by the *Itasca* show that the Electra was in the air twenty hours and twenty-five minutes. Amelia had reported being 200 miles out with no landfall, 100 miles out, that she was circling to pick up the island. The last message received by the *Itasca* was an incomplete position report, with the news that the aviators were moving north and south, trying to find the island. Then there was silence.

The uproar that greeted Amelia Earhart's disappearance was immense, with newspaper headlines like "LADY LINDY LOST!" More than a dozen vessels, including the aircraft carrier *Lexington* and the battleship *Colorado*, searched some 262,281 square miles of the Pacific—and found no trace either of the airplane or its crew. To match the intensity of the reaction to the Earhart disappearance, one would have to imagine a space shuttle vanishing in flight today.

The official story was that Amelia Earhart, having perhaps overshot Howland Island, circled in search, did not find land, and went down in the waters of the Pacific Ocean.

Nearly twenty-five years after the disappearance, CBS newsman Fred Goerner became aware of a story being told by a couple from Saipan. In 1937, the Japanese authorities on that island had a pair of white prisoners, one male, one female. They were aviators who were supposedly spies. The man was executed, the woman was reported to have died in prison.

After several years of investigation, marked by quiet hindrance from the U.S. government, Goerner produced his book *The Search for Amelia Earhart*, wherein he points out some tantalizing facts. The U.S. Navy searchers did not have the advantage of the full transcripts of Earhart's messages. Special transmission facilities had been set up on Howland Island, manned by naval, rather than coast guard, personnel. The original flight plan had called for a refueling stop at Midway rather than Howland Island.

The reason for these changes had to do with the Japanese Mandate—the Marshall, Caroline, and Chamorro islands. Originally Spanish holdings, they had been bought by the German Empire and lost to Japan in World War I. However, the League of Nations had given the Japanese mandate status only over the islands, on the condition that they not be militarized. But Japan became a virtual military dictatorship in the 1930s, and militarization of the Mandate had been underway since the 1920s. The seas in the area were closed to foreign vessels, and foreign planes were banned from island airports. When the League of Nations questioned these policies, Japan withdrew from the League in 1935.

American agents had tried to penetrate the area since the 1920s. A U.S. marine lieutenant colonel, Earl Hancock "Pete" Ellis, traveled in the area disguised as a German trader. His report in 1921 predicted the likelihood of a Japanese attack on Pearl Harbor—twenty years before the fact.

Perhaps, Goerner reasoned, the U.S. government had persuaded Amelia Earhart to fly over the Marshall Islands to the northwest of Howland Island to observe the major Japanese base at Truk. He discovered that the engines on AE's plane had been replaced during the long layover at Java with more powerful engines—the Electra could now move fast enough to make a swing over the Marshalls and still reach Howland at its normal ETA.

Goerner also points out that the naval report on which the search was based comments that Earhart and Noonan should have had clear weather all along their flight path. Yet one of the messages that the coast guard did not pass on refers to bad weather—and the only bad weather in the area was to the northwest.

Suppose the Electra had flown over Truk, gotten lost in the bad weather, and missed Howland? The last received message said the plane would head north and south. If the plane had headed north, hoping to make the British-held Gilbert Islands, it could have ditched in the Marshalls—where the crew would have been captured by the Japanese. It is important to note that five days after the Earhart disappearance, Japanese forces invaded China. If Earhart and Noonan were considered to have obtained Japanese military information, they would have been doomed.

Further research by Goerner has elicited testimony that in 1944, shortly after Saipan had been captured from the Japanese, a marine detachment was given the job of disinterring two bodies in a cemetery—the bodies of Amelia Earhart and Fred Noonan. These were brought clandestinely back to the United States.

The reason for the secrecy? The great shift in American public opinion. In the isolationist mood of 1937, any attempt to force the Japanese to give information on the whereabouts of Amelia Earhart would have been tantamount to a declaration of war with Japan—and would probably have resulted in President Roosevelt's impeachment, while discovery in 1944 of the body of Amelia Earhart, apparently executed for spying, would have resulted in a similar clamor against Roosevelt—in the midst of a difficult election. The American public has a short memory, and would have forgotten its mood of seven years earlier.

Certainly, despite Goerner's best efforts, the U.S. government has not been forthcoming with information or any evidence on the fate of Amelia Earhart.

However, while Goerner's theory has attained some popular appeal, it is not altogether accepted. Many point out that AE's World War I service as a nurse, tending the shattered casualties of that war, turned her into a dedicated pacifist. It would be ironic indeed to imagine her agreeing to take on a secret military mission for the U.S. government.

Perhaps the greatest irony, however, is Amelia Earhart's final destination, if Fred Goerner's hypothesis is to be accepted. This famous woman flier braved the Bermuda Triangle without result, and steered a course across the Pacific. Whether she crashed, was shot down, or captured and executed may never be known. But she remains one of the most famous and intriguing victims of the Dragon Triangle.

8

Mikakunin Hiko-Buttai

Potential dangers to shipping in the Dragon Triangle have been reported as coming from apparently controlled undersea activity with overtones of inner or outer space. Large and small ships have found themselves on collision courses with what were first known in Japan as *mikakunin hiko-buttai* (Unknown Flying Objects), now more popularly known even in Japan as UFOs.

In the Japanese islands, reports of UFOs are especially prevalent. The Japanese are attuned to spectacular natural phenomena such as earthquakes, typhoons, and tidal waves. For centuries they have observed strange objects in the sky but in other ages had considered them gods, dragons, ghosts, demons, or warning signs from heaven. In today's atmo-

117

sphere of interplanetary and space consciousness many of these concepts have metamorphosed into visitations from outer or inner space, and as such are accepted by a considerable proportion of the islands' population.

The number of UFO sightings received from different parts of Japan, its coasts and seaways, is noted by governmental sources (on the constant lookout for unscheduled foreign aircraft, under which heading UFOs would certainly qualify), as well as private organizations such as the Japan Space Phenomena Society. Records of UFOs are also kept throughout the world, awaiting the advent of a UFO which will, perhaps tomorrow, land, communicate, and be photographed in detail by Earth dwellers.

The question of UFOs has been an issue ever since pilot Kenneth Arnold on June 24, 1947, first sighted a flight of nine round "flying pie pans" over Mount Rainier in Washington. UFOs have so invaded public consciousness that a large portion of the earth's population believes not only that they exist, but that they have landed and made local human contact. Notwithstanding the thousands of reported sightings and contacts throughout the world, UFOs officially are still phantoms—phantoms that appear and disappear so suddenly that their appearances leave scientists and many laymen unconvinced as to their reality.

We have seen that ancient Japan had a deep and abiding interest in lights in the sky, lights which in many cases were incorporated into myths about dragons. However, some of the most ancient strata of Japan's archaeological heritage indicate the possibility of a more direct extraterrestrial involvement.

A very early period in Japan's cultural development was the Jomon Era, archaeologically dated at 3000 B.C., an era of cross-cultural ties with Polynesian cultures. Major artifacts of the era are small statues in human form made of earth, and later carved on soft rock. Early versions of these artifacts were small and very simple. However, by the middle of this period, the form starts changing to an entirely different style. The statues become bigger, and the figures depicted less human. The chests become larger, the legs bow, the arms become shorter, while the heads become larger, apparently covered by helmets. In fact, the whole effect is very similar to the creatures described by those who have experienced close encounters with UFOs. Specimens found in Lomoukai in Nambu province show helmets; and one statue, dated to 4300 B.C., shows what seems to be a perforated plate or breathing mask covering the lower face.

Ancient records of medieval Japan more than 800 years old mention a strange glowing object referred to as an "earthenware vessel" (a saucer?) flying through the night sky on October 27, 1180. An interesting parallel to a sighting with an "official response" is recorded from the year 1235, when mysterious lights in the sky were observed circling in the southwest from the campgrounds of General Yoritsume's army. When the general ordered an investigation, his wise men returned with the report that this was a natural phenomenon—the wind was merely causing the stars to sway.

A flying object supposedly in the shape of a drum rose from the inland sea in 1361. On numerous occasions, glowing objects looking like the full moon (sometimes in multiples) were beheld by the people. The old Imperial capital of Kyoto often reported seeing fireballs in the sky, one of which resembled a spinning red wheel.

This description tallies with a recent UFO sighting in the Chinese province of Kweichou on July 24, 1981. A star about the apparent size of the moon appeared, then a luminous tail developed, extending around the central star in a spiral manner. This case may involve the greatest number of people observing the same UFO. Witnesses numbered in the hundreds, from a simple tobacco farmer (who thought he had seen a flying dragon) to a university professor who turned his telescope on the object and discovered a row of portholes.

Perhaps the most recent "pre-saucer" UFO sightings in the area were in 1944 and 1945, the so-called foo fighters which dogged planes along the bomber routes to Japan and over the island of Truk. This phenomenon was also encountered by night bombers over Germany. Pilots reported seeing glowing blobs of orange, red, or white light by night, and silvery disks or globes by daylight. The name of the phenomenon comes from the old *Smokey Stover* comic strip, where one character would often mutter, "Where there's foo, there's fire." Foo may also be a play on the French word for fire, *feu*. The foo fighters were capable of tremendous speed, estimated at between 200 and 500 miles per hour.

In the European theater, the foo fighters were considered to be a Nazi secret weapon, developed to disrupt bomber radar or for psychological effect on bomber crews. After the war, while going through German secret files, Allied intelligence researchers discovered that a weapon called the *Feuerball*, or fireball, had been developed to confuse Allied radar.

How the weapon came to be employed in the Pacific theater was not explained. Also, postwar examination of enemy files unearthed reports of German and Japanese pilots who were pursued by foo fighters—and thought they were Allied secret weapons! The phenomenon was also dismissed at the time as a plasma discharge, an explanation very familiar to UFOlogists as ball lightning. But it is provocative to note that in the Pacific war, Allied bomber routes to Japan's cities passed over the heart of the Dragon Triangle.

In his book *UFOs and the Limits of Science*, Ronald D. Story lists what he considers the most baffling UFO cases. Six are

American, one British, one Iranian, and two take place in the Pacific.

On two consecutive nights, June 26 and 27, 1959, thirty-eight witnesses at the Boianai mission station on the shore of Papua New Guinea observed an incredible spectacle in the sky. Over a three-hour period three small UFOs and one large "mother ship" appeared and disappeared. At first Father Gill thought he had seen a very bright star over Venus. Then it descended.

Gill summoned Steven G. Moi and Eric Langford to watch the strange sight, and they were joined by more than thirty others at the shoreline. The glowing disks seemed to change colors, and figures were seen walking on a top deck of the huge disk—figures which appeared to be humanoid. A shaft of blue light coming up from the deck lit the figures, who also seemed to have a glowing field surrounding them. Some claimed to see a line of portholes in the mother ship as well.

On the next night, the mother ship returned, this time accompanied by two smaller units instead of three. The figures on the deck of the mother ship seemed to be at work constructing or adjusting something. As the craft floated overhead Father Gill waved to one of the figures who was looking down at him, and the gesture was returned. After several waves were exchanged and the vessel apparently waggled when Father Gill shone a flashlight at it, the figures went back into the UFO. They subsequently finished their work, remained in the area but considerably higher, and disappeared behind cloud cover approximately two hours after they had first been seen.

The second case, the Wellington-Kaikoura, is especially interesting, since it is one of the few where a UFO has been captured both on film and on radar. The radar sighting was sufficiently disquieting for the Royal New Zealand Airforce to place Skyhawk fighter bombers on the alert.

Two sightings took place, the first on December 21, 1981, the second (when filming took place) on December 31. The first observers were the crew of an Argosy cargo plane owned by Safe-Air Ltd. The aircraft followed a course along the eastern shore of New Zealand's South Island when the pilot, John B. Randle, reported white lights in the sky. Wellington Air Traffic Control's radar confirmed five unexplained objects in the air.

Approximately three hours later, another Safe-Air Argosy flying the same route was asked by Wellington Air Traffic Control to identify aircraft causing strong blips on their radar. A strong return was coming from about forty kilometers off the Argosy's port side. Captain Vern L. A. Powell and his copilot looked out the cockpit and saw the traveling light. Powell later reported: "Something is coming toward us at a tremendous speed on our radar. It has traveled some twenty-four kilometers in five seconds." To accomplish that flight, the object would have to be moving at 10,800 miles an hour.

Melbourne, Australia's, Channel O television station decided to do a news feature on the event, using reporter Quentin Fogarty, who happened to be vacationing in New Zealand at that time. Fogarty arranged for a camera crew, David Crockett and his wife, Ngaire, to accompany him for an air trip reconstructing the event. An Argosy air freighter took off from Blenheim, New Zealand, at 9:30 on December 30 for the flight to Wellington.

Arriving at Wellington, Fogarty interviewed air-traffic controllers, then rejoined the plane for takeoff at 11:46 P.M. At 12:10 A.M., December 31, Fogarty and his crew were filming in the craft's loading bay when the pilot alerted them that there were lights in the sky. For the next fifty minutes, pulsing balls of colored light appeared and disappeared. Crockett tried to film the display, but it was difficult. Wellington Air Traffic

Control confirmed that an unidentified blip was following the Argosy.

The plane landed at Christchurch, but at 2:15 A.M., on the return trip to Wellington, another flying light was discovered to starboard. The nearness of the object helped Crockett in filming it. It was described as having a clear dome over a saucer-like body. The UFO approached the Argosy as close as ten miles.

On the evening of December 31, Fogarty returned to Melbourne with the film—and Channel O had a sensation on its hands.

One of Fogarty's comments as he narrated in the background during the New Zealand UFO visitation was the phrase, "Let's hope they're friendly." Perhaps he had in mind an Australian UFO case from only three months before, where a pilot in the Melbourne area had a close encounter with a UFO—and was never seen again.

On October 21, 1978, Frederick Valentich was solo-flying his white and blue Cessna 182 single-engine from Melbourne to nearby King Island across the Bass Strait. At approximately 7:06 the twenty-year-old pilot noticed four lights above him, and radioed air-traffic controllers in Melbourne, asking if these were the landing lights of a military aircraft. He was assured no other planes were in the vicinity. The mystery machine passed over Valentich at least twice, after which the Cessna's engine began to malfunction. Valentich's last contact was to tell Melbourne that the strange object "was not an aircraft." This was followed by a strange metallic noise, and Valentich and his Cessna were gone.

Searchers spent four days combing the land, sea, and air for some trace as to what befell Frederick Valentich. All they found was an oil slick, which subsequent investigation dismissed, for it could not have been left by a small plane. The only clues to the mystery are in the transcript of the last six minutes of Valentich's flight, a conversation between the young pilot (code-named Delta Sierra Juliet) and the Australian Department of Transport Flight Service:

1906:14

DSJ: Melbourne, this is Delta Sierra Juliet. Is there any known traffic below five thousand?

FS: Delta Sierra Juliet, no known traffic.

DSJ: Delta Sierra Juliet, I am, seems to be a large aircraft below five thousand.

1906:44

FS: Delta Sierra Juliet, what type of aircraft is it?

DSJ: Delta Sierra Juliet, I cannot affirm, it is four bright, it seems to me like landing lights.

1907

FS: Delta Sierra Juliet.

1907:31

DSJ: Melbourne, this is Delta Sierra Juliet, the aircraft has just passed over me at least a thousand feet above.

FS: Delta Sierra Juliet, roger, and it is a large aircraft, confirmed?

DSJ: Er—unknown, due to the speed it's traveling. Is there any air force activity in the vicinity?

FS: Delta Sierra Juliet, no known aircraft in the vicinity.

1908:18

DSJ: Melbourne, it's approaching now from due east toward me.

FS: Delta Sierra Juliet.

1908:41

[open microphone for two seconds]

1908:48

DSJ: Delta Sierra Juliet, it seems to me that he's playing some sort of game, he's flying over me, two, three times at speeds I could not identify.

1909

FS: Delta Sierra Juliet, roger, what is your actual level?

DSJ: My level is four and a half thousand, four five zero zero.

FS: Delta Sierra Juliet, and you confirm you cannot identify the aircraft?

DSJ: Affirmative.

FS: Delta Sierra Juliet, roger, stand by.

1909:27

DSJ: Melbourne, Delta Sierra Juliet, it's not an aircraft, it is [open microphone for two seconds].

1909:42

FS: Delta Sierra Juliet, can you describe the—er—aircraft?

DSJ: Delta Sierra Juliet, as it's flying past it's a long shape [open microphone for three seconds] cannot identify more than it has such speed [open microphone for three seconds]. It's before me right now, Melbourne.

1910

FS: Delta Sierra Juliet, roger, and how large would the—er—object be?

1910:19

DSJ: Delta Sierra Juliet, Melbourne, it seems like it's

stationary. What I'm doing right now is orbiting and the thing is just orbiting on top of me also. It's got a green light and sort of metallic-like. It's all shiny on the outside.

FS: Delta Sierra Juliet.

1910:46

DSJ: Delta Sierra Juliet [open microphone for five seconds]. It's just vanished.

FS: Delta Sierra Juliet.

1911

DSJ: Melbourne, would you know what kind of aircraft I've got? Is it a military aircraft?

FS: Delta Sierra Juliet, confirm the—er—aircraft just vanished.

DSJ: Say again.

FS: Delta Sierra Juliet, is the aircraft still with you?

DSJ: Delta Sierra Juliet, it's [open microphone for two seconds] now approaching from the southwest.

FS: Delta Sierra Juliet.

1911:50

DSJ: Delta Sierra Juliet, the engine is rough-idling, I've got it set at twenty-three twenty-four and the thing is coughing.

FS: Delta Sierra Juliet, roger, what are your intentions?

DSJ: My intentions are—ah—to go to King Island—ah—Melbourne. That strange aircraft is hovering on top of me again [open microphone for two seconds]. It is hovering and it's not an aircraft.

FS: Delta Sierra Juliet.

1912:28

DSJ: Delta Sierra Juliet, Melbourne [open microphone
       for seventeen seconds].

[No official conclusion has been given for the strange
sound that interrupted the pilot's last statement before
he vanished from the sky—and from the sea.]

In propounding his theory regarding "vortices" of danger
in the equidistant parts of the globe and two additional ones—
located at each pole—Ivan Sanderson found data to indicate
mysterious disappearances in all of his Northern Hemisphere
locations. With the strange occurrences of 1978, perhaps the
vortex off New Zealand has now presented its first two
mysteries—and claimed its first victim.

Another possible vortex phenomenon was the air chase by
Iranian fighters near the capital city of Teheran early in the
morning on September 19, 1976. Besides civilians, witnesses
included high-ranking military officers and the crews of two
F-4 fighters.

The incident began after midnight, with phone reports to
Shahrokhi Air Force Base about a strange, bright light source
in the sky. The duty officer contacted the deputy commander
of operations, who, on checking for himself, observed a bright
light apparently seventy miles away. An F-4 Phantom jet was
scrambled to investigate. As the fighter moved within twenty-
five miles of the UFO, all instruments and radio went dead.
The plane broke off, and as it retreated, the systems became
functional again.

A second Phantom jet was scrambled, making radar contact
twenty-seven miles from the object and getting a return similar to the size of a 707 tanker craft. The UFO pulled ahead, and
the jet paced it, when suddenly a smaller light source

launched itself from the main UFO. As it approached the fighter, again all electromagnetic systems went dead. The F-4 dived, and the smaller UFO swung around and rejoined the main object, which was now proceeding south of Teheran. As the jet continued to follow the UFO, a second smaller object was ejected, this time on a trajectory to strike a dry lake bed. The object did not explode, but seemed to land softly, shedding light for some distance around its landing spot, then fading. The main object soon disappeared, speeding off into the night sky.

When the lake bed was investigated the next day, no traces of landing were found.

Perhaps the strangest Asian UFO incident occurred nearly forty years before the term "flying saucer" was invented. In 1908, in Russian Siberia, something came out of the sky and exploded on impact in the Tunguska river basin, near Lake Baikal. The blast was on the order of thirty megatons, and was detected as an earthquake on seismographs in the U.S. and in Europe. A fireball uprooted trees for miles around, and local settlements were destroyed. Glowing clouds spread, leaving Britain and Holland brightly lit at night. Thousands of people called to inquire if London was on fire.

The initial earthquake theory was discarded in favor of a meteor striking the earth. However, due to the remoteness of the region, the Czarist government never investigated, especially with the onset of World War I, revolution, and civil war. In 1927, Dr. Leonid A. Kulik, a specialist in meteors, led an investigation to Tunguska. His findings were surprising: there was no impact crater, and surviving witnesses gave a variety of descriptions—a fiery ball with a tail, a glowing cylinder. The accepted theory now was that Tunguska was the target of a small comet, which exploded on contact.

In 1947, a new interpretation was put on the facts. Could the Tunguska object have been an extraterrestrial craft whose

Right: Boiling sea bubbles indicate the eruption of an undersea volcano north of Iwo Jima.
(Photo: Wide World)

Below: The known volcanoes of the Dragon's Triangle. There may be hundreds of others.
(Photo: Wide World)

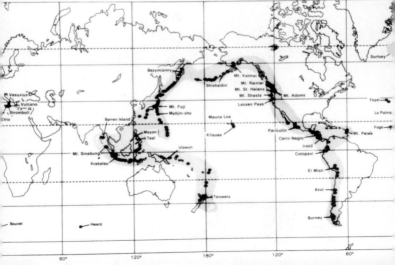

Above: Much the worse for wear, this carcass was netted by a Japanese trawler in 1977. Its measurements match those of the supposedly extinct plesiosaur. *(Photo: Fortean Picture Library, Wales)*

Below: A drawing rendered by a crewman aboard.
(Illustration from AP/Wide World Photos)

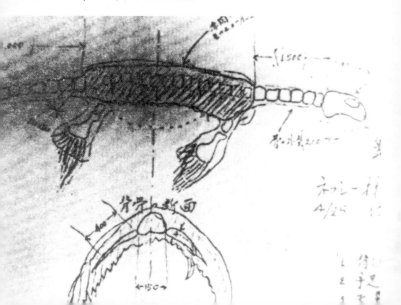

Above: The submarine *Kuroshio Maru*, translated as "Black Current," was named after the deep and dark underwater current that borders the Dragon's Triangle. Three *Kuroshio Maru* subs met their fate in the Dragon waters. *(Photo: Jane's Fighting Ships, Jane's Publishing Co., Ltd, London)*

Below: Prototype Buoy Tender of the *Kaio Maru*, weighing 500 tons. The *Kaio* left Myoyinsho on September 24, 1952, with its thirty-four crew members and vanished without any sign of wreckage. *(Photo: Jane's Fighting Ships, Jane's Publishing Co., Ltd, London)*

Above: This "Flower" class gunboat was a prototype for the *Fuyo Maru*, lost with all seventy-three crewmen on September 25, 1954, near Miyakejima.

Left: The *Geranium*, of the same model and type as this minesweeper, disappeared en route to Osaka on November 24, 1974. No trace of the crew members or fragments of the wooden vessel were ever found.

Below: After takeoff from Atsugi Airbase on June 26, 1955, the developmental prototype aircraft *F-3B* disappeared without a trace or distress signal. This Douglas *F3D-2* "Skynight" two-seater, all-weather fighter is one of the first of the operational *F-3B* designs.

(*Photos:* Jane's Fighting Ships, Jane's All the World Aircraft)

Below: On March 12, 1957, a United States Air Force *KB-50* disappeared between Wake Island and Japan without any sign of crew or wreckage. This Boeing *TB-50D* is the crew trainer of the same class as the missing tanker transport.

Foot: The United States Air Force *C-97* Stratofreighter was the freighter counterpart of this Boeing *KC-97-G* tanker transporter. It had a payload of over 40,000 lbs., a carrying capacity of over 50,000 lbs., and could be fitted to accommodate 134 fully equipped troopers or two tanks. On March 22, 1957, one of these aerodynamic giants disappeared off the south-eastern coast of Japan. No debris was ever found.

(Photos: Jane's All the World Aircraft, *Jane's Publishing Co., Ltd, London)*

Below: The Kawasaki *P-2J*, originally designated by NATO as a *P-2V*, was an antisubmarine aircraft fashioned after the Lockheed *P2-V*. How could such a sophisticated plane, equipped with search radar and warning systems, vanish without any kind of distress signal or detection as one did on July 16, 1971, within the Dragon's Triangle?

Foot: In April of 1968 a Soviet "Golf" class submarine was lost north-west of Japan. Although it was not nuclear-powered, this vessel carried both ballistic missiles and nuclear warheads of 800 kt and 7 MIRV of 100 kt. There were no survivors.

(*Photos:* Jane's All the World Aircraft, *Jane's Fighting Ships*)

Below: In September of 1974, a Soviet "Golf II" class submarine vanished south-west of Japan and was never found. The vessel had a crew of approximately eighty-seven men, twelve of whom were probably officers, and it was carrying both ballistic missiles and nuclear warheads of 800 kt and 7 MIRV of 100 kt.

Foot: This is a prototype of the "Golf II" class submarine that submerged in September of 1984, never to resurface. It carried ballistic missiles and nuclear warheads of 800 kt and 7 MIRV of 100 kt.

(Photos: Jane's Fighting Ships, *Jane's Publishing Co., Ltd, London)*

Top: In August 1980 the nuclear-powered Soviet "Echo I" class submarine, and in September 1984 a Soviet "Echo II," submerged forever into the Dragon's Triangle. Both "Echo I" and "Echo II" cruise missile subs are fueled by two nuclear reactors.

Above: In January of 1986 another nuclear-powered "Echo II" cruise missile ship drifted to the depths of the Dragon's Triangle.

Below: In 1970 a Soviet "Alfa" class nuclear submarine submerged in the Sea of Japan. The "Alfa" class submarine is propelled by a nuclear reactor and is equipped with eighteen torpedoes.

(*Photos:* Jane's Fighting Ships, *Jane's Publishing Co., Ltd, London*)

nuclear engine exploded? Thousands of small lustrous grains have been found in the Tunguska area—grains similar to the trinitite particles found at the Alamogordo atomic testing sites. Some investigators have found anomalous radiation readings, others have not. One commentator on the mystery suggested, "In the catastrophe along the Yenisey River in 1908 we lost a guest from the Universe."

Perhaps those guests are more frequent than we might believe. Using witnesses' accounts, we can trace the rough flight path of the Tunguska object. It came from the southwest, then changed course to the west, perhaps making for Lake Baikal, the huge, mile-deep freshwater source of Siberia. Was the Tunguska object attempting to avoid population centers? Was it trying to make a landing at or in the lake? Where was its original destination? Somewhere south and east of Siberia? China? Japan? the Dragon Triangle?

On Easter Island, far on the other side of the Pacific, a strange topographical anomaly can be found at the foot of Mount Rano Kau. A large, half-mile furrow is marked in the ground with obsidian, a black vitrified rock nonexistent elsewhere on the island. In line with this furrow is a small but well-defined crater. Could this be the site of another unrecorded hard landing? One can only speculate.

A spectacular UFO was sighted on November 17, 1986, by Japan Airlines pilot Kenjyu Terauchi, on a run to Alaska on a Boeing 747 cargo jet. Heading northward from Japan, the jumbo jet was followed at 37,000 feet by an enormous UFO for two periods, of twenty minutes and ten minutes, for approximately 300 miles of its flight path.

On the return leg of the transpolar route, the same plane, JAL Flight 1628, found a huge object outlined in glowing lights before them. Thinking he'd come in sight of a military aircraft, Captain Terauchi radioed Anchorage Flight Control to inquire if there were other planes in the area. The flight controllers assured him that his was the only traffic.

Coming from the front of the plane, the strange object approached within 1,000 to 500 feet, threatening a collision, then dove under the JAL jet. It then proceeded to follow from the rear. Captain Terauchi caught a look at the craft in profile and described it as looking "like a spaceship." Its size was huge, as large as "two aircraft carriers laid end to end," according to Terauchi, dwarfing the 747 jumbo jet.

The mysterious object created a detectable image on the JAL jet's weather radar. Blips indicating a craft near JAL 1628 were also noted on radar screens at Anchorage Flight Control and at the regional air force military control center as well.

Terauchi's two-man crew, a copilot and flight engineer, both saw bright lights tracking the plane. As a nineteen-year veteran JAL pilot, as well as a former fighter pilot for Japan's Air Self-Defense force, it is hard to believe that Terauchi would fabricate such a report with his flight crew. Indeed such reports often impact unfavorably on crew efficiency reports. Had the crew not felt it was their duty to report the incident, we would not be aware of this encounter today.

Crews of seagoing craft also encounter UFOs. Sometimes they hover for long periods, as one did over the *Taki Kyoto Maru*, a freighter sailing off the east coast of Japan, less than 200 miles from Kanazawa, on April 17, 1981.

Captain Usuda, when interviewed by the press at Kanazawa, reported that a UFO, of a round saucer shape and shining brightly, rose out of the sea in clear daylight and calm weather and first hovered near and then circled the 165-foot freighter. Captain Usuda described it as glowing with a blue light and stated that when it shot out of the ocean it caused a wave that almost swamped his ship. It caused another great wave, which partially damaged his ship, when it disappeared into the sea.

Captain Usuda, although preoccupied at the time with his terrified crew and his own concern for the ship's safety, noted that the time spent by the alternately hovering and circling UFO was about fifteen minutes. The UFO moved so fast around the ship that, except when it hovered, it could not be seen clearly—there was only a blur where it circled. Captain Usuda tried to radio for help but the transmitting equipment was jammed. He looked at the needles on the ship's instruments and they too were a blur, spinning with the same rapidity as the craft circling over the ship. He tried to guess the size of the UFO when it hovered and estimated that its metallic and glowing diameter was four or five times the length of his ship.

A curious result of the visitation was that it seemed to have affected time on board the *Taki Kyoto Maru*. After the UFO plunged back into the sea, the captain noted that the timepieces on board had lost fifteen minutes, the approximate time that the spacecraft (if that is what it was) had spent maneuvering around the ship.

A spokesman for the Japanese coast guard, Hoshi Isido, is reported to have observed, with some understatement: "Based on interviews . . . and the unusual structural damage . . . we do suspect that they encountered something very unusual. . . . Officially we are calling it an unidentified object, a simple UFO."

Perhaps the greatest source of speculation among investigators of UFO phenomena is the motive of the supposed intelligences behind UFOs. These break down into several hypotheses:

- *Observation:* Unidentified Flying Objects are either scout craft for a future military action, or, more benevolently, are considering us for communication with their own greater galactic civilization.

- *Indifference:* Occupants of UFOs have their own agenda, their own business to pursue on this planet. As long as humans do not hinder them in their pursuits, they ignore us as a man hurrying to the corner store ignores an ant hill along the way.
- *Colonization:* UFOs are servicing extraterrestrial bases beneath the water, or alternatively, they live here and are the products of an unknown terrestrial undersea population. This hypothesis has been proposed by the late Ivan Sanderson, who pointed to the numerous reports of glowing USOs (Unidentified Submarine Objects), and to reports of UFOs emerging from bodies of water. Indeed, Sanderson estimated that 50 percent of all UFO sightings take place over water. Even more conservative UFOlogists admit to a figure of 30 percent. Perhaps an explanation for the mysterious disappearances in certain areas of the world involves an intersection of major activity by underwater and surface cultures.

  One seeming objection to the colonization or civilization hypothesis is the fact that the underwater centers humankind has stumbled across (the Bermuda and Dragon triangles) are located in unstable earthquake zones. Seismic activity and volcanism would not seem to make these areas attractive for settlement—unless, of course, these areas had been *sought out* for those reasons. Volcanism might offer a cheap, undetectable source of geothermal power for an advanced civilization. And research is just beginning to accumulate serious data on the electromagnetic energy emitted by rock under tremendous pressure—pressure such as exists along tectonic fault lines. Perhaps these electromagnetic anomalies act as a sort of cosmic catapult to send the strangers' craft into the skies.
- *Portals:* Still another theory cites electromagnetic anomalies creating fault lines in the universe—space-time warps to other worlds, alternate universes, other dimensions, or the far past or future. According to this hypothesis, with the proper equipment, craft can traverse these warps in both directions. Occasionally, however,

these doors open for passing terrestrial air- and seacraft who enter these portals—on a one-way journey.

More recently, research in geophysics, that branch of geology investigating the forces which shape the earth, has suggested an even closer relationship between electromagnetic anomalies and UFOs. In this hypothesis, the glowing lights in the sky are created on Earth—in fact, *by* Earth, through the agency of tectonic forces grinding rock together at tremendous pressure.

Geophysicists have proven that in addition to the seismic shock waves that are broadcast by rock during an earthquake, electromagnetic radiation is broadcast as well. Radio receivers placed deep in mine shafts have caught broadcasts caused by underground blasts. Research along California's San Andreas Fault and in the USSR has also led to acceptance of electromagnetic discharges during earthquakes.

From ancient days, mysterious lights have been associated with earthquakes. In 1910, the geologist I. Galli noted the incidence of radiation in the visible spectrum connected with seismic activity in the U.S. Reports of such phenomena as auroras, columns, sparks, and balls of light were numerous. However, scientists remained skeptical of the "earthquake lights" until the mid-1960s, when photographic evidence of the phenomenon was obtained during the Matsushiro earthquake in Japan. Interestingly, it has been discovered that even small earthquakes can generate these lights, which need not appear near the quake epicenter.

Mountain peaks are often associated with strange light effects—the "mountain peak discharge." This phenomenon has been observed in several mountain areas, where the inhabitants have invested the occurrences with religious significance, such as the Chinese temple at the mountain Tai Shan, the Greek monastery located at Mount Athos, and the

American Indian veneration of areas like Mount Shasta as holy places. Wandering lights have long been a component of folklore (the "fairy lights") and it is possible that tectonically produced light forms, given religious significance in neolithic times, led to the construction of cyclopean structures such as Stonehenge and the Carnac standing stones in Brittany, both located in areas of tectonic instability. Various types of radiation—ultrasound, broadband radio, infrared—have been detected in these areas, and there are reports of static electricity discharges from the stones as well.

When Canadian psychologist Michael Persinger plotted reports of UFO activity against seismic events, he found that the localities coincided. His Tectonic Strain Theory suggests that UFOs are forms of visible light given off by "strain fields" of rock under heavy seismic pressure, related to piezoelectricity —electrical charges generated when crystalline rock formations such as quartz are put under pressure. Seismic pressure along a fault line could result in an "electrical column" extending into the atmosphere, which, by ionizing gases, would create a glowing form in the sky. If this ionizing column moves along the fault, the glowing form would move as well—giving the impression of a solid body flying through the air.

In Britain, David Devereaux was researching geological connections to light phenomena near Harlech, Wales, finding that sightings of mystical lights around the turn of the century coincided with a major fault line. Similarly, a 1977 series of UFO sightings in southwest Wales was correlated with earth faulting.

In 1981, Dr. Brian Bradley of the U.S. Bureau of Mines demonstrated in the laboratory that rocks under pressure could produce light effects. Slow-motion film of rock-crushing experiments showed the creation of light forms (not mere incandescent fragments of rock, but free-flying lights). Brady theorized that electromagnetic fields created by rock under pressure could act as "magnetic bottles" to give shape to the light forms.

Researchers have even found light emitted from nonpiezo-electric rocks, and experiments by David Devereaux and Paul McCartney have achieved light forms even underwater.

At this time, considerable discussion still rages on the strength of magnetic field needed to create large-scale light phenomena such as UFOs, and about the actual mechanism that causes radiation emission.

However, as Persinger points out, the visible spectrum may not be the only radiation emitted—there may possibly be radar UFOs and UFOs of deadly X rays, invisible to the human eye. Irradiation by such an unseen cloud could cause illness, nausea, or vertigo, and in some cases, might induce epileptic seizures or death through electrocution.

Could it be that in areas of heavy seismic activity—areas such as the Dragon Triangle—the very rocks of the earth itself emit bolts of energy powerful enough to kill crews or disintegrate air- and seacraft in their path? The U.S. government is presently experimenting with X-ray lasers as part of its "Star Wars" weaponry. Could the tortured rocks of the earth's crust already produce similar deadly radiation—naturally?

At this point in our knowledge of UFOs, any of these preceding hypotheses and many more can be advanced and defended. This is because UFOs, as their name implies, are *unidentified* objects. They may represent a new form of aerial navigation—some recent test planes bear a startling resemblance to the popular conception of UFOs. However, it must be remembered that unidentified flying objects have been observed by all cultures for many millennia. Until a UFO lands and its living occupants are interviewed, it cannot be established where UFOs come from or why they come to Earth.

In addition to ghost ships, UFOs, and sea serpents, there is even ghost radar to be found in the Dragon Triangle. Ships and planes passing west of Okinawa along the Nansei Shotō island chain have long been aware of a curious radar disturbance in the area. Frequently there appears on radar a large moving object which changes position, dissipates, or vanishes as ships or planes approach it. Is it a surfacing submarine or marine animal that moves into and out of the radar screen? Or is it an immense geophysical or interdimensional force, invisible to the eye but still detectable on radar? Whatever it is, the area has been indicated on admiralty charts as a warning and as a possible source of disturbance in the area. This mystery is widely known in maritime circles, where the phenomenon has been accepted and even nicknamed the Galloping Ghost of Nansei Shotō.

While the ghost of Nansei Shotō is apparently harmless, there are other, more worrisome, ghosts to be found in the Pacific—and especially in the Dragon Triangle.

9

The Shaking Land, the Restless Sea

Another Japanese earthquake tradition is that of the *namazu*, the gigantic catfish that lives in the mud beneath the earth. This creature is given to pranks, and is restrained only by the Kashima god. Armed with a magical keystone—a rock with divine powers—the Kashima god keeps the *namazu* under his control, and the earth stays still. Should the Kashima god relax his guardian vigil, however, the *namazu* escapes his power and impudently thrashes his body, causing earth tremors.

In 1855, in the so-called month without gods—the time in October when the deities gather at a distant shrine—a serious earthquake struck the city of Edo (now Tokyo). There was widespread damage, and thousands died. According to the popular belief of the time, the Kashima deity's absence had freed the *namazu* to create havoc. Woodblock prints showing the angry deity returning, wielding his mighty keystone, the *namazu*'s caperings for forgiveness, and the creature's final ignominious fate were widely distributed to cheer the populace, and still exist today. Some even show a social consciousness, satirizing government officials and carpenters and artisans who would make a profit out of the disaster.

In the second century A.D., a Chinese scholar with a practical turn of mind invented the first earthquake detector. This early genius, known in history as Cho-ko, came to the conclusion that waves rippled through the earth from a tremor zone, just as they radiate from a stone dropped into a pool. Since an earthquake wave had a direction, it could be detected with the right equipment. By establishing several detectors, he could determine the source of the tremor by triangulation.

Cho-ko's detector took the form of a round, drum-shaped body, eight feet in diameter, with dragon carvings spaced equally around it. Each dragon held a ball in its mouth, and below awaited eight small statues of frogs, each looking up open-mouthed to catch the ball should the dragon drop it. Cho-ko's theory was that, as his earthquake waves passed, they would rock the mechanism, dislodging the ball from the mouth of the dragon in line with the tremor.

Although crude, his machine was actually quite ingenious. Cho-ko was lucky, however, in that on the occasion when a ball dropped, a report of an earthquake in that direction came in a few days later. In consequence, the Imperial Government appointed Cho-ko as the first official seismologist.

We know today that there are much more titanic forces at work than the tomfoolery of a gigantic denizen of the sea. And though we have better detection equipment than Cho-ko's dragons and frogs, modern science is still vague on predicting tremors and helpless at preventing them.

The European explorers who survived the turbulent passage around Cape Horn into the relatively calm seas beyond could not have given the newly discovered ocean a more misleading name. The Pacific is anything but a peaceful ocean. Its storms are the most violent in the world, and its shores regularly rumble with seismic activity. From the west coasts of both Americas, across Alaska and the Aleutians, to the east coast of Asia and down into Indonesia, earthquakes and volcanoes create a zone known as the Ring of Fire.

The Dragon Triangle brings its own triangle of catastrophe to the midst of this dangerous ring, since two arms of the Dragon Triangle represent some of the most seismically active areas on earth. The situation has been described as a geological time bomb ticking away beside one of the most densely populated areas on the planet.

Japan's home islands represent a land area approximately the size of California, yet five times the number of California's inhabitants live there. Since mythological times, the area has suffered major earthquakes. Here is a listing of the major seismic activity known to Westerners:

China, 1556—Very little is known about this earthquake, which was said to devastate three provinces and take approximately 800,000 lives.

Japan, 1596—An offshore earthquake created a tidal wave, a tsunami, which completely destroyed one island, killing more than 4,000.

Japan, 1737—A 200-foot-high tsunami came in from the Pacific to devastate Japan's northern coastline.

Japan, 1793—The volcanic island of Unsen exploded, accompanied by earthquakes. The island completely disappeared. More than 50,000 people died, and volcanic pumice was ejected onto the sea in such quantities that it was thick enough to walk on.

Indonesia, 1815—A 13,000-foot volcano, Tambora, erupted for a week, ejecting thirty-six cubic miles of solid material—the single greatest recorded eruption on Earth.

Japan, 1857—Tokyo was destroyed by earthquake and by fires started by charcoal-cooking braziers, which spread through the city's wood-and-paper houses.

Indonesia, 1883—The island of Krakatoa was reduced by 50 percent in a volcanic eruption. Subsequent tsunamis, 115 feet high, struck Java and Sumatra, with a loss of 36,000 lives. These seismic water waves were so powerful they actually circled the earth twice. Ash from this eruption blocked sunlight and lowered world temperatures for the following year, resulting in the Year Without Summer for many northern locations. New England was struck with summer snowstorms.

Japan, 1891—Severe tremors attacked 4,600 square miles, more than half the country's area. In thirty seconds, more than 7,000 people died.

Japan, 1896—A tsunami between 80 and 150 feet high struck the eastern coast of Japan, drowning 26,000 and destroying 100,000 homes.

Taiwan, 1906—More than 6,000 buildings and 1,300 lives were lost in an earthquake.

China, 1920—One of the most devastating earthquakes in history attacked Kansu province, killing 200,000.

Japan, 1923—The "Kwanto earthquake" leveled Tokyo and Yokahama, killing 143,000 and leaving 500,000 homeless. An indirect effect of this tremor was the final discrediting of Japan's civilian government. After this point, the militarists took over, and started Japan on its march toward Pearl Harbor.

Japan, 1927—A quake almost equal to the Kwanto earth tremor destroyed 14,000 buildings and killed 3,000.

Japan, 1946—An undersea earthquake shook the island of

Honshu and caused enormous tidal waves, wiping out fifty coastal towns. Two thousand died, and 500,000 were left homeless.

Hawaii, 1946—An earthquake in the Aleutian Islands near Alaska produced a tsunami which traveled 2,300 miles to destroy the city of Hilo, Hawaii, with the loss of 160 lives. Property damage was estimated at $25 million, a more expensive loss than that suffered in the Japanese attack on Pearl Harbor.

Japan, 1952—Three hundred miles off the Japanese coast, in the midst of the Dragon Triangle, oceanic bubbling was discovered by local fishermen. It turned out to be the birth of a new island, called Myojinsho, in the Bonin island chain. The island rose and sank several times, emitting lava "bombs." This outburst may be connected with the loss of the *Kaiō Maru No. 5*. In addition to the eruption, tide gauges on an island seventy-five miles north of the site registered the impact of a tsunami.

Hawaii, 1960—A tsunami from an earthquake in Chile roared across the Pacific at jetliner speed to strike the city of Hilo, causing the death of sixty. The seismic water wave continued on to Japan and the Philippines, to claim another 400 people.

Alaska, 1964—The largest earthquake recorded in North America struck Anchorage, Seward, Valdez, and Kodiak Island. More than one hundred lives were lost, as well as almost $1 billion in property damage. The quake's tsunami struck coastal towns as far away as Oregon and California.

China, 1976—Earthquakes in Tangshan took at least 650,000 lives.

The theory behind the recurrent seismic activity in this area involves more than a simple fault line where rock pressure builds up until it is released violently. It is a hypothesis which involves the entire earth, one that was considered incredible by respectable geologists as recently as twenty-five years ago.

From the beginnings of the science of geology, there has been conflict between those who believed that the earth's surface has been reshaped catastrophically (by the biblical flood, for instance) and those who believed that changes were accomplished more gradually, uniformly, over hundreds of millions of years. Throughout the nineteenth century, the uniformitarian (from uniform change) viewpoint held sway, though there were those who pointed to strange anomalies, such as the fact that the eastern coast of South America could fit into the western coast of Africa like a piece in a giant jigsaw puzzle. The only way to explain the two continents' separation (and the Atlantic Ocean in between) was to resort to a tremendous catastrophic event.

In 1858, author Antonio Snider hypothesized that all the future continents began as a single supercontinent, which broke apart early in prehistory. This notion was amplified in 1879 when George Darwin, son of evolutionist Charles Darwin, suggested that the moon had been spawned by a vast discharge of material from the earth, creating a vast void in the planet (which became the Pacific basin) and causing the continents to drift.

The notion of continents set adrift by unimaginable catastrophes, however, was too much for most uniformitarian geologists. In 1885, Eduard Suess attempted to reconcile the two positions, preparing a map that showed how all the southern continents could be fitted together in a mass he called Gondwanaland. But it was Alfred Lothar Wegener who truly championed the theory in the beginning of the twentieth century. His hypothesis added fossil evidence, explaining the spread of certain types of creatures whose presence is in areas now separated by oceans, as well as further geological evidence. Not only did continental coastlines fit together but other land characteristics, such as mountain ranges, also lined up when the continents were joined. Wegener also suggested that the resistance of the sea floor against moving continents might create mountain ranges such as the Rockies and the Andes.

From 1912, when he first unveiled his theory, until 1930, when he died on an expedition to Greenland for more proof, Wegener fought a good fight. However, with Wegener's death, the theory of continental drift was essentially buried until the 1950s, when the invention of the astatic magnetometer allowed geologists to study the magnetism of ancient rock layers.

This "fossil magnetism," however, provided disturbing readings. English rock strata seemed to indicate that England had once been much closer to the equator. India had once been located far down in the Southern Hemisphere, and had moved north. Either the magnetic poles had shifted, or the continents had.

The ocean depths also provided a possible mechanism for this movement. An enormous underwater ridge was discovered in the mid-Atlantic, apparently a dividing line between the separated continents. Princeton University geologist Harry H. Hess proposed the theory that the midocean ridges were not cracks in an expanding Earth, as some had hypothesized, but part of a self-regulating system. They were hot spots where material from the asthenosphere, the more plastic portion of the earth's mantle, pushed up through the lithosphere and the earth's crust at the thinner ocean floors. This new material made the sea beds expand.

Essentially, the sea bed and lithosphere below it acted like a giant plate. If a continent was embedded on the plate as well, it too would move, as if it were on a conveyer belt. Where plates came in contact, one would sink below the other, to be remelted by the heat of the earth's core. The site of such sinkings, or subductions, was marked by oceanic trenches, often topped with volcanoes beyond the trenches, as melted material welled up through the cracks in the victorious plate. After years of discussion and argument, most geologists now accept this idea of what are called tectonic plates. A number of major plates with continents embedded have since been identified, as well as some smaller ones.

The area of the Dragon Triangle is actually the meeting place of three tectonic plates—two major ones, the Eurasian and Pacific plates, and the much smaller Philippine plate. As the Pacific plate presses against the Philippine and Eurasian plates, it is subducted, creating the Ogasawara Trench. As the Philippine plate presses against the Eurasian, it too is subducted, forming the Ryukyu or Nansei Shotō Trench. These trenches roughly form two of the arms of the Dragon Triangle.

As the leading edge of a tectonic plate is subducted, the rock does not go quietly to its doom. It catches, grinds, develops pressure—and causes earthquakes. Plotting the epicenters, the focal points of the tremors, at subduction sites gives a ghostly outline of the downgoing plate, sloping steeply into the earth. Generally speaking, the deeper the epicenter, the more disastrous the earth tremor. This is why China suffers such seismic devastation. The final death throes of the undersea plates that start subduction in the trenches east of Japan are felt under the Chinese mainland. However, tremors affect more than just the localized area of the quake. The whole earth reverberates like a beaten gong.

As the focal point of three tectonic plates, Japan—and the waters to the south and east—experience considerable seismic agitation. Besides earthquakes, there are the further phenomena of volcanoes and seismic water waves.

Volcanic activity behind subduction zones is easily explained. As one crustal plate is forced downward by another, the friction between the two heats rock to the point where it erupts through any weak points in the surface plate. The result is an arc of volcanoes behind the ocean trench that marks the subduction, which sometimes turns into an island chain. Japan itself is a massive construct of volcanism.

Shock waves created by either an earthquake or a volcanic eruption can cause a tsunami, which literally translates from the Japanese as "harbor wave." These are sometimes referred to as tidal waves, but they have no connection with the tides. Tsunamis are essentially the water-borne shock fronts from seismic disturbances. Perhaps the best descriptive term for these waves comes from the Spanish-speaking countries of western South America. There, seismic water waves are called *maremotos* (seaquakes), as opposed to *terremotos* (earthquakes).

Traveling deep in the ocean water, tsunamis may even be undetectable. As the shock waves from the 1946 Aleutian earth tremors headed for Hawaii, they did not move as great walls of water. Ships at sea rode over them without noticing anything out of the ordinary.

It is only when these shock waves reach shallow water near shorelines that they are deflected upward and begin to gain height. They take the form of a breaker, as most waves do on shorelines. Friction slows the bottom of the wave, so that the top falls forward. However, the amplitude of these waves can be several stories—or even hundreds of feet—tall.

Shallow water also slows tsunamis. Through deep water, these shock waves travel as fast as 750 miles an hour. At the shoreline, friction can cut that speed to fifty miles per hour. However, as one can well imagine, the destructive power of tons of water moving at such speed makes the potential for loss of life, destruction of property, or even annihilation of an island obvious.

Another point to consider is that the narrower the passage to shore, the more violent a seismically generated wave be-

145

comes. A case in point is Lituya Bay, a fjord in the Alaskan panhandle approximately 150 miles north of Seward. Surrounded on three sides by cliffs, the bay measures three miles long by one mile wide.

A geologic fault lies across the mouth of the bay, and when major earthquakes shake the area, massive avalanches from the cliffs plus displacements of the bay floor can result in enormous harbor waves. On July 9, 1958, a major tremor shook ninety million tons of rock from as high as 3,000 feet off the surrounding cliffs and into the bay. The resulting wave that swept through the bay and out to sea caused some minimal property damage and claimed only two lives due to the fact that it took place in such a remote location. We should be glad this is the case. Scientists surveying the area found that this wave had surged to a height of 1,740 feet—making it the highest wave from any cause ever recorded in history.

Although science has now formulated theories to explain these phenomena, and even equipment for accurate measurement of their power, mechanisms for detection before the fact are still far in the future. Therein lies the peculiar danger for mariners and even air pilots in areas such as the Dragon Triangle.

The closest man-made equivalent to the release of energy in a volcanic explosion is the detonation of a nuclear warhead. In addition to smoke and steam, volcanoes eject tephra, broken material of the volcano itself, ranging in size from microscopic ash particles to chunks of rock 200 feet wide. Volcanoes are also known to discharge "bombs," pieces of semihardened lava, with the force of artillery shells. These are clearly physical dangers for any passing ships or planes.

Eruptions are also known to affect air currents and weather. In recent eruptions in the Dragon Triangle, smoke, ash, and hot air were vented 6,000 feet into the air in 1969, 8,800 feet in 1974, and 12,000 to 13,000 feet in 1952. Atmospheric phenomena accompanying serious eruptions include thunderstorms with lightning and cyclonic winds, a definite peril for sea-borne or airborne traffic.

Of special danger to seagoing vessels are the seismic water waves, the seaquakes which rock the ocean after seismic activity. The danger may pass unnoticed in deep water, but the area of the Dragon Triangle is dotted with small islands, reefs, and shoals, and in this shallower water, the wave's deadly effects are experienced. A ship caught broadside by a wall of water could be capsized and sunk in seconds, hurled down into the deeps by the power of tons of water.

Witnesses to tsunami activity have passed on incredible reports of anchored vessels wrapped in their own anchor chains, after being spun on their long axis like a rolling pin. There are stories of ships being hurled into cliffs, or simply being swamped and never seen again. A ship taken unawares by the sudden rush of a tsunami has an excellent chance of simply disappearing, without even time to radio an SOS.

Another phenomenon associated with volcanism and earthquake activity is that of the boiling sea. Here is an eye-witness account of the offshore occurrences during an 1854 earthquake:

> We felt the first shock at 9:15 A.M.; it was very strong . . . at the end of five minutes the water in the bay swelled and began boiling up, as if thousands of springs had suddenly broken out; the water was mixed with mud . . . and hurled itself upon the town and the land to either side with shocking force.

From this description, it seems possible that a large dis-charge of underground gas accompanied the earthquake. Some theorists have even hypothesized that underwater tremors could become considerably more dangerous with a gas discharge. Consider the effect of an enormous bubble of poisonous, possibly volatile gas being released from the ocean floor. The shock of its passage through the water would be added to the seismic waves. And what would happen when this monstrous bubble reached the surface and burst? At the very least there would result a tsunami, accompanied by severe turbulence in the water in the area where the bubble emerged. A ship caught in such an area would be swamped and immediately dragged down by underwater eddies resulting from the massive disruption.

Before this is dismissed as sheer hypothesis, mention should be made of reports from the research ship *Melville*, which, on October 11, 1987, experienced giant bubbles of gas bursting against its hull. The hull rang and the ship nearly capsized. It was later determined that an undersea volcano had erupted directly below the ship's position.

Perhaps the crew and scientists of the *Melville* were lucky in the amount of gas emitted by the volcano. Their case might be similar to that of the *Kaiō Maru No. 5*, which disappeared so mysteriously in the locale of an undersea volcano. Perhaps it was a greater eruption or outgassing that took that research ship to the bottom with hardly a trace.

Seismic activity also has more subtle effects than these gross movements of the earth's crust or the ocean's waters. In some unknown way, it also affects the invisible force we know as magnetism.

Earthquakes in the Dragon Triangle have been known to cause magnets to lose their properties—or regain them. During one earth tremor in the mid-nineteenth century, witnesses noticed that nails attached firmly to magnets fell off as if the magnetic field had been interrupted. An even more interesting episode comes from a ship in Tokyo Harbor during the great earthquake of 1923. Weird magnetic effects were observed both before and after the earth tremor, including control dials spinning wildly. This is a familiar phenomenon of both the Dragon and Bermuda triangles—a phenomenon which may be explained when Japanese and other researchers probe deeply into the magnetic component of seismic activity.

For the Japanese people themselves, living in a perpetual earthquake zone seems to have engendered a certain fatalistic attitude. This has been noticed by Western observers of many of the seismic disasters which have struck the islands. Homeowners simply stared, struck dumb, as their property burned to the ground, rather than fighting the fires.

Perhaps this attitude can also be perceived in the communities which resume normal lives in areas of active volcanism. Photographs of children wearing hard hats on the way to school because their route comes close to a vent known to eject stones are more than mere picturesque filler material for news magazines. They represent a way of life forced on a society with too many people and not enough land.

By no means, however, do the Japanese wantonly disregard warnings of volcanic or seismic activity. Indeed, they are probably the most earthquake-conscious people in the world. Recent eruptions on a volcanic island in the Dragon Triangle caused the evacuation of thousands. The Japanese government in 1978 adopted a measure for spending more than $3 billion a year for earthquake preparedness measures.

There has not been a major seismic experience in Japan for some years. However, there is worry that such an experience is overdue. One researcher, in reviewing Tokyo's seismic history since A.D. 818, proposed that the area has suffered earth tremors at the magnitude of eight or higher on the Richter scale once every sixty-nine years, give or take thirteen years. Since the last major tremor to strike Tokyo was in 1923, this deadline is getting much closer.

Seismologists even have a possible epicenter for an earthquake in the region: the Tokai area on the coast south of Tokyo. Although there have been minor tremors from time to time, the region has not experienced a major earthquake since 1854, when the rice paddies, orchards, and fishing villages were devastated, with a loss of 3,000 lives. Despite occasional shakings (one of which cost twenty-five lives), seismic tension has been building up without real release. Such signs of strain as a one-foot drop in the coastline have been detected. The area has become built-up as well; some six million people now live in 170 cities through this once-rural area. A cataclysmic earth tremor could cause untold loss of life and damage to property. And if the shock continued up the fault line to Tokyo, the catastrophe would be seriously compounded.

It is for reasons such as these that the Japanese conduct regular earthquake drills, to the point of declaring September 1 National Disaster Prevention Day—the same date as the 1923 earthquake.

A visible sign of Tokyo's turbulent seismic history can be found in the cliffs overlooking Tokyo Bay. Disturbances over the centuries have raised the cliffs, which are slightly broken by the action of the waves to create small beaches—which in turn are raised considerably above sea level by the next seismic tremor. A number of these stratified former beaches can be seen on the cliffs as the land has been upthrust.

Similar rising of land mass and sea bottom has been a continuous phenomenon in the Dragon Triangle, causing danger for mariners. It takes place all across the Pacific, however. In the Fiji Islands, Resolution Bay, named for Captain James Cook's ship, is now too shallow for such a ship to take harbor there.

However, for every instance of land which rises, there are also instances of land which subsides, sometimes sinking beneath the sea. The 1964 Good Friday earthquake in Alaska gives striking evidence of that phenomenon, the largest example on record. Sixty thousand square miles of land and sea bed were uplifted by this earth tremor, while 48,000 square miles sank. Kodiak Island was so affected that one of the few buildings which withstood the shock, a government office, now has its first floor underwater at high tide.

The Alaska tremor affected these land masses by only a few feet. But is it possible that entire cultures could have been wiped out by the subsidence of their homelands? Tantalizing evidence has been found in the widely scattered island cultures of the Pacific.

10

The Uncertain Islands

As the largest body of water on this planet, the Pacific Ocean has the scope to hide incredible mysteries, and the power to create amazing marvels. The highest ocean wave was sighted in the mid-Pacific, by the U.S. naval tanker *Ramapo*. The ship was sailing to leeward (i.e., downwind) of a storm, when the officer on the bridge spotted an enormous wave behind the vessel. By sighting through the crow's nest of the mast, to the top of the wave, he set up a simple problem in geometry to determine the wave's height. The straight line through the crow's nest and the angle of the deck gave two sides of a triangle. All the officer had to do was calculate the third side. His answer made the wave out to be 112 feet tall. Wind-driven waves ten feet high are considered heavy weather.

The vast spaces of the Pacific allow scope for unprecedented weather disturbances. The cyclonic storms or hurricanes, known in the area as *typhoons* (from the Chinese *t'ai fung*—"a great wind"), have an area of literally thousands of square miles in which to grow, with no great land masses to hinder them. The greatest wind speed ever recorded was in a cyclonic storm which made an anemometer revolve at 187 miles per hour. At that point, either the machinery broke or the equipment was literally blown away. Meteorologists have estimated cyclonic winds in excess of 200 miles per hour. Some typhoons, it is believed, pack winds of up to 250 miles per hour.

The greatest weather losses of World War II were due to a typhoon which struck Admiral Halsey's Third Fleet as it made a rendezvous for refueling. Unknown to the fleet's weather officers, the fleet was sailing directly into the path of a typhoon. The center of the storm passed so close to the aircraft carrier *Wasp* that the newly developed radar for the first time recorded the eye of a storm. Airplanes were torn from moorings and catapults and twisted into debris, or torn loose to roll across decks, spreading fire and wreckage. Ships heeled over to a degree greater than seamen had ever believed possible.

Three destroyers heeled over too far. Water poured down their funnels, and they sank to the bottom. In a period of less than an hour, and in a space of over 100 miles, the three ships went down. An additional six craft were damaged, and over 800 men were lost.

When a typhoon finds an island in its path, gigantic wind spirals can batter the land for as long as twenty-four hours. But this is not the only dangerous effect of typhoons. The low barometric pressure of the storm center can cause the ocean to rise. The spiraling cyclone winds can literally "pile up" water into a huge dome. When this dome of water reaches a shoreline, it greatly elevates the tides—sometimes by as much as thirty feet. When this force is added to the already pounding waves, man-made structures can be collapsed completely, towns destroyed, and in the cases of low-lying islands, vegetation removed and the population wiped out.

Little wonder that in ancient times such storms were attributed to the gods themselves.

Lesser cyclonic disturbances, which become waterspouts over the sea, are dangerous for smaller ships, but there are reports of major vessels steering right through them with little or no damage.

Although there is no major land mass for the 10,000 miles between Asia and North America, there are innumerable small islands, often forming chains or archipelagoes. These are the tops of submerged mountains rising from the Pacific ocean bed, which in some cases would surpass Mount Everest in height. Most of these islands are of volcanic origin, which often shows in their round shape. Even the large islands of Hawaii, with their irregular contours, are merely massive dome volcanoes or groups of volcanoes, whose original shapes have been eroded by the sea.

Examining a map of the Pacific, we see evidence that island groups seem to come in arcs. It is theorized by geologists Jason Morgan and J. T. Wilson, the founder of the plate tectonics theory, that the islands were formed volcanically as plates passed over "hot spots" in the earth's crust, creating as it were a line of volcanoes which rose above the sea surface. Expanding this theory, Morgan further hypothesized that the "island arcs" actually show the direction of the tectonic plates for the past 100 million years. The bend in the arc represents a change of course for the Pacific plate—initiated forty million years ago.

This theory may be further proved by the discovery of hundreds of *guyots* or seamounts, underwater mountains whose flat tops do not breach the ocean's surface—at least, not today. Dredging samples have detected traces of coral, which can only grow in warm, shallow surface water. Also, some seamounts are fairly close to the surface. The Erben Guyot is a seamount approximately one-third of the way between San Francisco and Hawaii. It is only 350 feet below water level.

The flat tops of the seamounts would seem to have been shaped or eroded by surface forces. However, tectonic activity may be involved as well. The farther seamounts are located from a volcanically active area, the lower and flatter they are observed to be. Perhaps in moving away from the hot spots of their birth, these former islands no longer had the power to sustain themselves above the waves.

In the cooler Northern Pacific, islands are almost solely volcanic. The numerous "jimas" of the Ogasawara or Bonin chain are all stacks—eroded volcanoes. In warmer waters, Pacific islands fall into three general classifications, which also seem to indicate different stages in an evolutionary process.

The first stage is the volcanic island with a fringing coral reef. Coral is not a rock, but rather the protective exoskeleton of a polyp type of sea animal, which thrives in the shallow waters around islands. Examples of islands with fringing reefs are Tahiti, Nauru, and Rarotonga.

The second classification or stage is the island with a barrier reef. Here the central island and a quiet lagoon are encircled by a wall of coral, with breaks to allow ships in. It is theorized in this case that the actual mountain is subsiding. However, as the original island shrinks, the coral ring at the old coastline continues to grow, maintaining the island's original girth, almost like a fossil record. Examples of such islands are the Truk group and Ponape, whose cyclopean ruins are believed to be subsiding into the sea.

The third class of island is the atoll, a circular island made completely of coral, with a still-water lagoon in the center. Coral thrives best in agitated water, such as the sea side of an atoll, rather than in the quiet lagoons, where silt from the now-vanished island chokes growth. One might call this the graveyard of an island, although many atolls are populated. Such familiar World War II locales as Wake and Midway islands, as well as Eniwetok, the site of atomic testing, are atolls.

Heights of islands vary greatly. The Truk group has islands which tower to 1,000 feet above sea level. In the nearby Marshall Islands, an atoll chain, the highest "peak" is thirty-five feet.

The danger to small, low-lying land masses in the midst of a large ocean can be illustrated by a legend from the island of Pukapuka in the Cook Islands. A small island with little commercial use, it has been left in the care of the London Missionary Society. However, the island has a history preserved in an oral genealogy stretching back twenty-two generations. Ethnologists Ernest and Pearl Beaglehole in the 1930s recorded the epic story, including a "te mate Wolo"—the great death that occurred in the seventeenth century. Apparently, the natives became so depraved in that era that they began looting the graves of their ancestors. Angry gods sent a tsunami which reduced the population from thousands to two women and fifteen men. In more recent memory, a tidal wave swept away Toka, a small island nearby, in 1914.

Such history nearly repeated itself at the island of Majuro. Praised by the author and poet Robert Louis Stevenson as the "Pearl of the Pacific," this is where he spent his later years, writing, among other stories, *Treasure Island*. Majuro is actually a collection of three small, narrow coral atolls connected by causeways. It is only 600 feet long and wide enough for only one transverse road. When a tsunami swept over the island in 1979, Majuro was completely devastated, and has yet to recover fully. Had the wave been a bit larger or more powerful, the entire population of this island might have been exterminated—and perhaps even the island itself might have been destroyed.

The Tuanaki Islands lying southeast of Rarotonga represented, according to visitors in 1842, a pleasant South Seas preserve uncorrupted by contact with Western ways and diseases usually brought by whaling crews and other seamen. But when missionaries were sent to the islands in 1844, they were unable to locate them, as the islands had disappeared, along with their happy inhabitants who thereby missed a chance to become civilized.

In February 1946 observers on a British warship, the HMS *Urania*, saw an island rise out of the Pacific 200 miles southwest of Tokio. The island's two cones were about 50 feet high, and the ocean at that point about three miles deep. The island covered more than a square mile. The British Admiralty named the island after the *Urania*. Nevertheless, the island submerged two months later.

Maps of the world, and especially maps of the Pacific, abound in island locations with question marks, or markings such as "doubtful." These are islands which have been discovered and had their latitude and longitude noted, but other ships have never found land at those locations.

Less critical or careful cartographers leave these islands, but omit the dubious signs. As Henry Stommel, the author of *Lost Islands*, relates, he found a large-scale globe in an airline office with the location "Morrell Island" marked in quarter-inch letters at the northwestern end of the Hawaiian Islands. The "discoverer," Benjamin Morrell, had a fair amount of fame in his lifetime as the author of several popular books on his voyages of exploration. There is some indication that he fabricated some of his adventures, but there is also the possibility that Morrell's navigation was so bad that his 1823 landing actually took place on the island of Cure, far to the east.

Stommel attributes the discovery of many dubious islands

to faulty navigation. While seamen have "shot the sun" to get the declination for latitude, the problem of accurately determining longitude remained until the late eighteenth century and the development of dependable marine chronometers to estimate the distance from the Prime Meridian at Greenwich. Until then, celestial navigation depended on careful notation of the lunar cycle, much calculation, and considerable luck. However, this rough method involved possible inaccuracies of up to 15 degrees—more than a thousand miles. Other mistakes in charting islands may be the result of mirages. A U.S. submarine near the Strait of Formosa in 1944 sighted a convoy of supposedly Japanese ships and prepared to attack. But when the attack was ready, the ships suddenly vanished—from one moment to the next. The nearest convoy was more than 100 miles away. The attack target was a mirage.

Today's satellite navigation systems bring this method back in amended, and considerably more accurate, form. Even in the days of chronometers, however, inaccuracies could creep in. The regular gain or loss of a few seconds could accumulate disastrously on long voyages, when comparisons with clocks in civilized ports could not frequently be made. There are stories of ships returning from long travels with their chronometers as much as two hours off the correct time. This would, of course, mean that any longitudinal locations would be dreadfully inaccurate.

With nearly 500 years of mariners' voyages across the Pacific, numerous islands were discovered and erroneously located, creating phantom islands hundreds or even thousands of miles from the true landfalls. Some were outright fantasies, such as the Islands of Gold and Silver, Rica de Oro and Rica de Plata, supposedly located to the east of Japan. A search for these rich islands ended the work of Spanish explorer Sebástian Vizcaíno, who was mapping and preparing the coast of California for colonization. This interrupted project was only resumed more than 150 years later, so that Spanish, and later, Mexican presence in the area was not strong—leading to an American annexation.

The Spanish, incidentally, continued to search for the islands until 1768, when they finally abandoned the project. However, a Spanish sea captain did make landfall on an island in the supposed area in 1801, resulting in the location being kept on some maps and atlases as late as 1922.

Similarly, during the great land grabs in the Pacific before the Civil War, numerous claims were entered for guano islands in what came to be called American Polynesia. The reason for the claims was for guano companies to get protection of their islands from the U.S. government. Thus, claims were presented to the State Department, and, to get them in the public record, were also leaked to a newspaper, the *New York Tribune*.

In the newspaper's printed list of forty-eight islands, we see such familiar names as Malden, Christmas, and Howland islands. However, modern cartographers find numerous misspellings in the names, and serious inaccuracies in the latitude and longitude. Some may be clerical errors, such as switching an island from east to west longitude, for instance. However, the final assessment was that there were a total of twenty-one doubtful islands in the list.

Vincent Gaddis, the author of *Invisible Horizons*, notes that in 1858 the United States government listed over a dozen islands in the South Pacific and claimed that they belonged to the United States "under the Act of August 18, 1856." But, as none of these islands was ever surveyed or correctly located on charts, the United States lost territory which apparently had not existed in the first place.

Other islands reputedly discovered in the South Pacific were named and entered on charts as Duke of York, Grand Duke Alexander, Monks, Favorite, Dangerous, and Massacre, all ephemeral, having disappeared after they were first located. One wonders who explained to the Duke of York that an island named after him had somehow been lost.

In 1885 an island in the Tonga group rose almost 300 feet above sea level and seemed to be established permanently with a diameter of two miles. The island, named Falcon, suddenly disappeared but reappeared in 1927 and now seems stationary at 100 feet above sea level.

Due to the confusion in maritime circles about appearing and disappearing islands, in 1875 Captain Sir Frederick Evans, the hydrographer in charge of the British Navy's admiralty charts, looked into the matter of doubtful islands in the Pacific and banished 123 specks from his maps—including three which represented actual land.

Navigational errors, however, do not explain landfalls and discoveries of large bodies of land, made by able mariners, which cannot be duplicated. For instance, in 1687 British privateer Edward Davis came upon an island to the west of South America. In his 1699 book on voyages, the navigator Dampier states:

> Captain Davis told me lately that . . . about five hundred leagues from Copiapó on the coast of Chili [sic] (Chile) in latitude 27 degrees south he saw a small sandy island just by him; and that they saw to the westward of it a long tract of fairly high land tending away to the north-west out of sight.

This area became known as Davis Land, and excited much comment in the eighteenth century that it might be a part of the Antipodean Continent, the balancing land mass to Europe that many expected to find in the Pacific.

When Jacob Roggeveen sailed into the area in 1722, he found no trace of Davis Land—the only land he did find was

Easter Island, which by no means could be confused with the description Davis gave.

However, there are Spanish records that report in 1576 a landfall by a navigator, Juan Fernández, who had gone far into the Pacific to avoid the impeding currents on a journey from Callao to Valparaiso. After a month's sail, encountering a land with "the mouths of very large rivers from whence and from what the natives intimated and because they were people so white and well-clad and in everything so different from those of Chile and all Peru," Fernández deduced he had come upon an entirely new land, perhaps a new continent.

Thus, we have two mariners encountering a fairly sizable land mass, with reports of inhabitants, in a span of more than 100 years. Less than fifty years after the latest report, this land had disappeared. In 1912 a British vessel, the *Glewalon*, sighted an island off Easter Island. When a Chilean training vessel sailed to verify, they spent three weeks searching—and their soundings revealed ocean depths of nearly two miles. Sarah Anne Island, northwest of Easter Island, survived on the maps for almost a century. In 1932, a search for the island, which would have been in the path of totality for a solar eclipse in 1937, found only empty sea.

Hunter Island was an inhabited island, named after her discoverer, the captain of the whaling ship *Donna Carmelita*. Landing there in 1823, Captain Hunter found intelligent and fairly civilized Polynesians who had the strange custom of amputating the little finger of the left hand at the second joint. The location of this island was carefully noted, as was the nearest land, called Niaufu, or Tin Can Island. However, other voyagers to this area never saw the island.

The St. Vincent Islands were discovered in 1789 by the Spaniard Antonio Martinus, and as late as 1824, a Catholic priest reported living on these inhabited islands. He described them to the sailor and author Benjamin Morrell as well wooded, with good harbors. Morrell spent a month searching the area in 1825, but found only discolored water 120 fathoms (720 feet) deep.

In 1860 a U.S. warship, the USS *Levant*, disappeared between the 133rd and the 138th meridian west and the 15th and 20th parallels north. It was supposedly wrecked on an uncharted island. When a U.S. warship and cruiser was sent to investigate, neither the USS *Levant* nor the island was found.

Then there is the disappearance of Tuanaki, near the island of Rarotonga. Several sightings were reported by whalers between 1840 and 1860, and an attempt made by a missionary ship to reach the island in 1844 failed. Missionaries reported that the island had disappeared, and in 1876, two ships passed through the island's position without sighting anything.

In the New Hebrides Islands, a U.S. naval officer, Commander Meade, was sailing through the area aboard the USS *Narragansett* in 1872–73. In his Remarks Book, he notes that a nearby inhabited volcanic island erupted and disappeared, and that "the survivors saved themselves with great difficulty."

Similar eruptions on the Japanese island of Unsen sent it beneath the waves in 1793 with a loss of 50,000 lives, and a tsunami inundated the island of Uryu-Jima in the Ogasawara chain in 1596. Four thousand died, the few survivors making their way to the mainland on fishing vessels. More recently, 13,000 abandoned the island of Oshima when a volcano became active.

Considering the alternate risings and sinkings of the ocean bottom of the Pacific, one understands the fear of land dwellers in the Pacific islands that their land may fall back into the ocean, especially the great cities and ports built at sea level in the circling lands called the "Ring of Fire." And it is here that the volcanic eruption has been increasing in recent years.

Against such a background, where whole islands can vanish, the disappearances of a few vessels or planes seem almost pedestrian, although, for an island nation like Japan, extremely serious. All that can be stated with certainty is that no one knows how—or when—the titanic forces of the Pacific, and the Dragon Triangle, will next unleash themselves.

11

Sunken Lands and Vanished Civilizations

Just as geology has its uniformitarians and catastrophists, so too does the study of history. And once again, the catastrophist viewpoint is as popular with orthodox historians as it was with orthodox geologists thirty years ago. The orthodox view of history offers an orderly progression of cultures and learning, from the early Egyptian and Mesopotamian civilizations through Greece and Rome, with a setback in the Dark Ages, followed by the resumption of learning in the Renaissance and the triumph of today's culture.

Essentially, this view is fixed on Western civilization, with a slow addition of concurrent development in the Far Eastern cultures. However, there are entire cultures—those of Minoan Crete, the Indus Valley, and the Maya, for example—about which very little is known. Even when there are records extant, they are often unreadable.

Orthodox history is especially resistant to the idea of the more simple ancestor cultures having anything like modern knowledge; and often implements of higher technology are displayed under the convenient catchall category of "ritual objects." That is where one researcher found constructions which turned out to be ancient electrical batteries. Another archaeologist discovered a perfect lens in the ruins of Nineveh—1,900 years before such lenses were supposed to be possible. His find was dismissed as a piece of jewelry.

A philosopher at MIT, Thomas Kuhn, has used the term *scientific paradigms* for the hard-and-fast notions scientists have developed regarding the way the world operates. Now and then discoveries are made which are so large and fundamental that they necessitate a paradigm shift. Once upon a time, for example, it was *known* that the earth was the center of the cosmos. Time and space were once viewed as absolutes. But since paradigms shift, established ideas about the Way Things Are must be brought into line with an emerging body of information which contradicts the paradigms.

For many years, there has been an emerging body of information—from folklore and legend, from language similarities on both sides of the Atlantic, and more recently, from ancient sites emerging from the waters of the Caribbean, underwater ruins near Madeira in the Atlantic, off the coasts of Spain and Morocco and evidence of a "pre-flood" civilization in the Canary Islands—that there once had been a developed civilization which sank beneath the waves: Atlantis. Even with this collected proof, the response of orthodox historians ranges from skepticism to outright hostility.

How then do we deal with the whispers and hints of an ancient civilization in the vastness of the Pacific?

If anything, scientific hostility to the idea of a Pacific lost continent is even stronger than that to Atlantis. Geology gives no indication that parts of the Pacific sea bed had ever been above water, and continues to hold to the position that any such changes had to occur over millions of years, at a rate hardly to be considered change at all. Alterations on a global scale take place in a cosmic time frame, not a human one. It is a paradigm of conventional science that geological changes such as continental drift, or the subsidence of land area beneath sea level, occur over millions or tens of millions of years.

But on a map of the Pacific you can find a huge area known as Oceania, in which are strewn a multitude of coral atolls and volcanic islands. Some of them are isolated specks; most are grouped in chains and archipelagoes. Many of their names carry a romantic resonance: Tahiti, Samoa, Hawaii, Tonga.

But these islands contain more than the suggested locale of adventure novels. There exists on them an abundance of phenomena, archaeological and cultural, which resist rational explanation when conventional notions of the region's geological and social history are applied. These phenomena suggest alternative theories, unorthodox but not new, whereby the phenomena in question emerge not as mysterious anomalies, but as legacies of a little-known past.

The most familiar locale of these puzzles is Easter Island. Also known as Rapa Nui, Easter Island is an isolated speck thousands of miles west of Chile. It was discovered by Jacob Roggeveen, a Dutch explorer, on Easter Sunday, 1722, while he was searching for Davis Land, a large archipelago which had been described at that location some years earlier. Of the archipelago, Roggeveen found no trace.

Thanks in large part to the work of explorer and author Thor Heyerdahl, the world is familiar with Easter Island's most remarkable enigma: the enormous statues, called *moai*, which dot large areas of the landscape. They are elongated figures, showing torsos and heads, and while they vary in size, even the smallest of them can fairly be called monumental.

The stone from which the *moai* were made came originally from a huge quarry at a site called Raru Raraku. Here they were carved. Then the statues, up to sixty feet in height and weighing as much as thirty tons, were transported over distances as great as ten miles, where huge stone platforms, called *ahus*, awaited them. The *moai* were then lifted and set upright on the *ahus*, and additional elements made of red stone, often characterized as topknots, were placed on top of them, suggesting a growth of reddish hair.

The culture of the Easter Islanders of the present era does not employ the sort of technology required to move and set up such immense carvings. There is no written history to which scholars might go for answers; indeed, the culture employed no written language. When asked about the *moai*, islanders are vague; they tend to explain the remarkable feat of moving enormous statues over rough terrain without destroying or damaging them in terms of magic. Magic spells or incantations, they are likely to say, were used to make the statues "walk."

At another Easter Island site, Vinapu, there is a partially destroyed wall constructed of great slabs of rock skillfully laid together, with smaller stones used to fill in niches. Archaeologists have noted a striking similarity between the ruins at Vinapu and those found in Peru at Cuzco, Machu Picchu, and elsewhere.

In *Aku-Aku*, his book on Easter Island, Heyerdahl has this to say about the *moai* and other cyclopean relics of Rapa Nui: "One thing is certain: this is not the work of a canoe-load of Polynesian wood-carvers. . . . The red-haired giants with the classical features were made by seafarers who came from a land with generations of experience in maneuvering mono-liths."

Another question has been raised concerning the *moai* of Rapa Nui. There are at the Raru Raraku quarry a large number of stone blocks and statues in varying stages of completion, suggesting that there was an abrupt cessation of all work. Something made these ancient artisans suddenly abandon their work. We can only guess at a cause.

The island of Ponape, or Pohnpei, is the largest island in the eastern Caroline archipelago, which is in turn the largest archipelago in Micronesia, consisting of about five hundred islands. It lies 5 degrees north of the equator, roughly 1,000 miles northeast of New Guinea. The island, of volcanic origin, has a population of roughly 20,000. The population is neither industrial nor especially industrious. They do not carve or work in stone, nor have they ever manifested any great tech-nological expertise.

And yet on the coast of Ponape can be found the ruins of a stone city of remarkable size and complexity. It is called Nan Madol (variant spellings include Nan Modal and Nan Metal). The visible remains cover 175 acres. The city was built of gigantic elongated blocks, or "logs," of basalt crystal, a vol-canic rock which is particularly hard and heavy. These logs, most of which are from three to twelve feet in length, some even approaching twenty-five feet, were quarried at a site about thirty miles distant. The logical inference is that rafts were used to move them to the location of the city.

Nan Madol consists of a number of enormous platforms, laid out over the native coral in a checkerboard pattern. On these were constructed a palace, a feast hall, temples, living quarters, tombs, vaults, mausoleums, and other edifices. A massive sea wall protected the city from the ocean, and a sea gate in that wall gave marine traffic access to the port. The basalt logs were laid down crisscross fashion, rather like an enormous American-style log cabin but made of stone. No mortar was used to cement the slabs together.

The city appears to have been designed in three parts: the lower city where lived the king and his court and the nobles; the upper city in which the temples and priests were to be found; and the massive surrounding walls, containing the vaults, tombs, and mausoleums.

No one knows how old Nan Madol is. An estimate of roughly 1,000 years was made by the Smithsonian Institution, but it could easily be substantially older. The technique of carbon dating will not work with stone, and, as on Easter Island, there is no written history, one that we can decipher.

Native legends attribute Nan Madol's construction to two brothers, Olsihpa and Olsohpa, who are said to have arrived on the island in a large canoe and completed the building in a single day, using magical incantations which caused the great stones to fly into place. There are indications that objects of worship at the temples included sea creatures such as turtles and eels, but essentially the culture of which Nan Madol was a part seems to have vanished completely, again, as in the case of Easter Island, while in the midst of quarrying stones for new construction.

However, the bare fact of the existence of such a marvel at such a location must give rise to speculation, such as that of John MacMillan Brown in his book *The Riddle of the Pacific:* "The rafting over the reef at high tide and the hauling up of these immense blocks, many of them from five to twenty-five tons in weight, to such height as sixty feet must have meant tens of thousands of organized labor . . . yet within a radius of fifteen hundred miles from this as a center there are not more than fifty thousand people today."

There have always been rumors of another, sunken city, in the waters near Nan Madol. A German author, Herbert Rittlinger, wrote in 1939 that divers had observed well-preserved streets, pillars, monoliths, and vaults, and that Japanese divers had actually brought up quantities of precious metals and jewels from the site.

More recent and concrete evidence exists. Dr. Arthur Saxe, in a 1980 paper, *The Nan Madol Area of Ponape: Researches into Bounding and Stabilizing an Ancient Administrative Center*, writes of finding a set of boulders in a straight single-line formation. Other divers exploring these waters have reported finding pillars and inscribed basalt stones. As large and complex as Nan Madol appears above sea level, the possibility must be weighed that part of an even greater metropolis has disappeared beneath the surface of the Pacific. A city of such magnitude seems disproportionately large in the context of a small and thinly populated island such as Ponape.

In the Mariana Islands can be found the remains of enormous structures called *lat'tes*. These consist of upright monoliths, arranged in two parallel rows of from four to six stones, surmounted by comparably huge capitals.

On the island of Tinian stand the ruins of the House of Taga. This is formed by a series of truncated pyramidal pillars, measuring eighteen feet in circumference at the base and fifteen feet at the top, standing twelve feet high. The capitals are from five to six feet in diameter. When the Spanish who first explored the island asked about the builders, the natives, or Chamorros, replied that it had been done by "the people who came before."

On the Isle of Pines, off the coast of New Caledonia, were found mounds of sand and gravel. When they were subjected to examination, it was discovered that they contained pillars of cement made of a lime-mortar compound. The pillars were from forty to seventy-five inches in diameter, and from forty to one hundred inches tall. There is no clue as to their original purpose.

In Polynesia, the Marquesa Islands have a scattering of *ahus*, huge stone terraces reminiscent of those platforms on which *moais* were placed on Easter Island. Herman Melville writes of them in *Typee*, commenting on their great size, the evident skill employed in their construction, and their obvious antiquity.

Thor Heyerdahl, in *Aku-Aku*, describes a series of walled hilltop fortifications on the tiny island of Rapiti. He investigated one, known by the present-day inhabitants as Morongo Uta. Once upon a time, a previous culture built and lived in them, but no one has done so within the memory or oral history of the current natives, who know nothing of the people who were responsible for them.

On the island of Yap are a number of stone embankments and terraces resembling the *ahus* of the Marquesas, as well as pillars, stone-paved roads, and the ruins of what were probably meeting houses.

Truncated pyramids known as *marae* can be found in the Society Islands, Mooréa, Raïatéa, Maeva, and Bora Bora.

The *Bounty* mutineers who originally settled on Pitcairn Island found it uninhabited, but discovered four quadrangular platforms, one of which overlooked the only usable harbor and had a statue at each corner. They destroyed the statues and disposed of the remains in the ocean.

In the Kiribati group is a remote and barren spot of land called Malden Island. At this site are found the remains of a group of stepped and truncated pyramids, together with paved ways that descend to the sea.

About 1,000 miles due south of Malden Island lies Rarotonga, the largest of the Cook Islands. On Rarotonga there is an ancient paved road which makes a circuit of the island. It is called the Ara Metua.

Structures have been found on many islands of Melanesia

including the northern New Hebrides, Santa Maria, the Banks Islands, Fiji, and Ysabel in the Solomons.

In none of the instances cited is there any indication of a link between the contemporary populations and the shadowy builders whose work still stands, though usually ruined and covered over with jungle growth. They strongly hint at the existence of a long-vanished culture whose ability and desire to build are not reflected in the societies that have supplanted them. Orthodox science, confronted with their existence, can only admit to lacunae in its knowledge of this area's past.

The societies of Oceania transmitted knowledge, history, and myth orally. They did not use written languages. But only on Easter Island were found, inscribed on stones and carved into tablets of a wood not native to the island, examples of a written language which has not yet been translated.

These are called *rongo-rongo* tablets. We lack an equivalent to the famous Rosetta Stone, by means of which the Egyptian hieroglyphs were first understood. It has been said that when Westerners first reached the island a handful of the indigenous population were able to read the *rongo-rongo* tablets, but if such knowledge were extant at that time, it has by now disappeared completely.

We do know that the script is boustrophedon—that lines are meant to be read alternately from left to right and from right to left, "as the ox plows," as were early European and Asian scripts. We also know that there is a very strong resemblance between the written symbols found on Easter Island and those of another, ancient culture, that of the Indus Valley of what is now Pakistan.

The Indus Valley culture is thought to predate the historical culture of India. Its two chief cities, Mohenjo-Daro and Harappa, are known to have been in existence at about 4000 B.C. These cities were built of brick and featured elaborate systems for the transportation of water and the disposal of waste. At roughly 3500 B.C., however, the culture vanished, probably destroyed by barbarian invasions from the north. The factors that make for technological sophistication are, unfortunately, seldom a match for the brute force of uncivilized hordes bent on conquest.

What makes the undeniable similarity of these languages extraordinary is partly the fact that the Indus Valley source had ceased to exist over five millennia ago; but also that Easter Island and the cities of Mohenjo-Daro and Harappa are virtually diametrically opposite each other on the globe. There is literally no point of land anywhere on the globe that is more distant from this island than the Indus Valley.

That a society such as that of Rapa Nui might on its own, and in isolation from other cultural influences, have created a system of writing such as that found on the *rongo-rongo* tablets is difficult to credit; that the symbols so created would bear such a resemblance to another language created half a world away seems incredible, although such is the case. In Mohenjo-Daro and other ancient cities now in Pakistan, this writing has been preserved on seals of clay or metal, while on Easter Island the same system of writing was inscribed on hardwood tablets. Most of these have been lost, looted or destroyed through the centuries. The script, which may be syllabic or hieroglyphic, is almost exactly the same but equally unreadable and, unless someone finds the key, will probably remain so.

Linguistic similarities have also been noted between the Maori of New Zealand and the Indian Quechua of Peru. The following similarities either crossed the Pacific east-to-west or west-to-east, or perhaps originated on a large Pacific land mass now covered by the ocean.

English	Maori (New Zealand)	Quechua (Peru)
between	pura	pura
chieftan	kura	kuraca
love	muna	munay
skin	kiri	kara
sweet potato	kumara	kumara
mutilated	mutu	mutu

On a tiny Oceania atoll called Faraulep, the Thilenius South Seas expedition of 1908 recorded a list of numeric symbols, representing numbers of extremely great magnitude: 100,000, 200,000, 300,000, through 1,000,000, 3,000,000, 5,000,000, 10,000,000, and even 60,000,000. The practical use of such numbers for a primitive people on a tiny and isolated island is difficult to conceive.

As in the case with the archaeological relics, we have no known historical explanation that accounts for the presence of fragments of written language in areas inhabited by nonalphabetic peoples. Certainly the two sets of phenomena might well be supposed to have a common source—a culture of considerable attainments and of a high degree of civilization.

However, the lack of a recorded history creates a frustrating vacuum of concrete knowledge of that culture, notwithstanding the profusion of artifacts which they have left. Some additional light may be shed on these elusive people by looking at some of the myths and legends of the territory. As in the remnants of written languages, there are some remarkable and suggestive similarities.

The arrival in Peru of the Spanish conquistadors led by Francisco Pizarro did not, as might well have been expected, create in the Amerind natives the shock of an encounter with something utterly undreamt of. The Spaniards were in fact thought to be legendary beings called *viracocha*—members of a light-skinned, fair-haired race possessing great knowledge and power who, according to the prevailing oral tradition, had visited Peru long ago and had promised that they would return.

Legends exist in the Maldive Islands about the Redin, or "ancient people." These were described as fair and blue-eyed, and they are credited with having built the ancient temples and cities there.

The legend of the Mataora in New Zealand similarly describes an early people of great powers and attainments. New Zealand contains huge and complex drainage systems dating to the distant past which presuppose not only great skill in building and design, but also the availability of a vast supply of labor and the logistical expertise to properly house, feed, and manage them. It is to the Mataora that the making of these marvels is ascribed.

There is a myth in Polynesia that tells of Wakea, a prophet or teacher, who is described as fair and brown-haired, who arrived in the islands at some time in the distant past. He is said to have come with others who resembled him on three great ships with huge sails and oarsmen.

According to its oral tradition, Easter Island was peopled by two races, called the long ears (*hanau eepe*) and the short ears (*hanau momoko*). The long ears were generally taller, fairer, and tended to have lighter hair, often of a reddish color. They were supposedly more industrious and usually dominated the short ears, until the latter rebelled.

Heyerdahl, in *Aku-Aku*, tells of meeting with islanders who claimed to be descendants of the long ears, and who in fact had the appropriate hair coloring and other physical characteristics. These individuals proudly stated that their ancestors had been responsible for the *moai* and other artifacts for which their island is known. The *moai*, of course, were originally topped by large stone topknots, suggestive of red hair, and the statues exhibit the long earlobes that gave the *hanau eepe* their name.

The incidence of fair-skinned, light-haired travelers in the mythic traditions of so many widespread places leads to a supposition that there actually were such people at some time in a prehistoric past. Their skills in construction and the use of stone were considerable, and their ability as navigators and seafarers would indeed seem to have surpassed those of Western civilization of the time.

One glaring problem manifests itself in considering such a sophisticated culture: how is it possible that a civilization so advanced and accomplished could have vanished so utterly from the earth, leaving only the fragmented and elusive bits and pieces of evidence we have discussed?

In dealing with that question, we must confront the problem of uniformitarianism; in this case, in geology. While geologists have at last accepted the catastrophist theory of continental drift, they still cling to the notion that this movement, or land subsidence, inevitably took place only over periods of time measured in millions of years. The destruction occasioned by earthquake, volcanic eruption, or tidal wave is essentially minor against their chosen time scale.

However, history does provide some examples of adventurous seagoing cultures being weakened or wiped out by single seismic catastrophes. The destruction of Port Royal in 1692 cost Britain her richest city in the Caribbean, as well as an all-important base for English buccaneers. Built near a fault line, one-third of the city slipped into the sea, while the remainder was battered by a tsunami. In more ancient times, a volcanic eruption at Thera destroyed a large port city on that island, while lashing the shores of Crete with a tsunami. The result was the decline and disappearance of Minoan civilization.

Could an earthquake have shaken the central base of an

adventurous, light-skinned maritime race into the sea, leaving small colonies to wither and be absorbed into native populations? Might a prehistoric Krakatoa have destroyed an island kingdom that had once unified Oceania?

As recently as 12,000 years ago, Ice Age glaciation had reduced the sea level by some 600 feet. Islands like the Hawaiian chain and large portions of sea bottom in what are now Indonesia and Malaysia would have been dry land.

Myths about cataclysms are common to many, if not most, peoples in all parts of the world. Witness the story of Noah. Similar legends are as common as archaeological ruins among the islands of Oceania.

Let us consider Easter Island. The oral traditions of the indigenous population on the island say that Easter Island is actually the only trace above sea level of a great land called Hiva, the rest of which now lies under the surface of the Pacific Ocean. As the pronunciation of Hawaii is correctly Havaii, the similarity to Hiva is of interest. "Hiva" is also the name given by the Maoris of New Zealand to their land of origin, formerly to the east, near the Marquesas, where the memory of a lost or sunken land mass still exists. There is also the legend of Hotu Matua, a demigod who brought learning and magic to Rapa Nui from his homeland when that place sank into the sea.

On the island of Yap there is a small village called Gatsepar, whose inhabitants every year bring tribute to islands situated hundreds of miles away, as a means of avoiding earthquakes and tempests and other destructive natural occurrences.

These traditions are normally classified as legends. But it should be borne in mind that when Jacob Roggeveen discovered Easter Island in 1722, he had been searching for Davis Land—a large, sandy archipelago that had been described with some precision by John Davis at that very location some years earlier.

Macmillan Brown, in *The Riddle of the Pacific*, asserts, "It is impossible to account for the remains of the old Easter Island civilization except by the existence of a submerged archipelago at the place where Davis Island was sighted."

Easter Island is also known to lie on a major fracture zone, an area where the tectonic plates that underlie the earth's crust come together, and consequently, a focus for seismic activity. When it made its round-the-world voyage, the American nuclear submarine *Nautilus* took note of a very high but still unidentified undersea peak quite close to the island. And more recently, Professor H. W. Menard of the University of California has discussed not only an important fracture zone in the vicinity of Easter Island, but also the discovery of a very suggestive and huge bank or ridge of sediment.

The floor of the Pacific is strewn with seamounts—huge cones with flat tops, some or many of which may have been islands. And even in historic times, as recently as 1836, an island called Tuanahe, south of the Cook group, disappeared.

The sunken traces of structures in the waters near Nan Madol are an indication of subsidence which may have inundated the greater part of a large city. Even considering only what we can see of Nan Madol above the surface, from where could the huge number of laborers necessary to complete such an undertaking have come?

While each single element of evidence in itself does not carry sufficient weight to shake the foundation of established scientific dogma, an accumulation of such items becomes collectively more and more impressive.

Other relevant and highly suggestive facts can be gathered from the study of old maps. One of the most noteworthy is the Piri Reis map, which dates from 1513. Drawn in Turkey, this map purports to be based on much older charts and maps "drawn in the days of Alexander." The map shows quite a bit of detail of the coastline and interior of South America—a remarkable amount, indeed, in view of the fact that Columbus's initial voyage predated this map by only twenty-one years, and that no European had penetrated the interior or west coast of South America.

But the most interesting aspect of the Piri Reis map did not come to light until quite recently, when a copy came into the hands of a retired U.S. Navy captain, Arlington H. Mallery. It was he who observed that the outline of a land mass at the southernmost end of the map bore a striking resemblance to the contours of Antarctica—as they would appear if not covered by its present two-mile thickness of ice.

Other maps show Antarctica to be comprised of two distinct land masses. Only very recent technological developments have enabled us to determine that these ancient mapmakers were correct about this, and about their detailed depiction of this little-known region.

Other maps roughly contemporaneous with the Piri Reis map have been brought to light, such as the Oronthius Fineaus map of 1531, the Gerardus Mercator map of 1538, and the Ptolemaeus Basilia map of 1540, all of which suggest a familiarity with the contours of Antarctica as it would be without ice.

We know that glaciers advance and recede, and that what are now polar zones were not always so. But if we operate from the viewpoint of the uniformitarian, Antarctica was ice-shrouded for countless millennia before men first began to draw the most primitive kinds of maps, let alone explore the farthest reaches of the planet.

Only if we take the catastrophist position that, at some time in very recent geological history, the prevailing climate of what is now the south polar region was quite different can we arrive at a rational explanation for the existence of these maps.

In his book *Maps of the Ancient Sea Kings*, Charles Hapgood writes: "The evidence presented by the ancient maps appears to suggest the existence in remote times, before the rise of any of the known cultures, of a true civilization of a comparatively advanced sort. . . . This culture at least in some respects may well have been more advanced than the civilizations of Egypt, Babylonia, Greece, and Rome. In astronomy, nautical science, mapmaking and possibly shipbuilding, it was perhaps more advanced than any state of culture before the eighteenth century of the Christian Era.''

A civilization of such advanced scientific and technical achievements that only in the last two centuries have we begun to match or surpass them may have lived well before the advent of any recorded history available to us today. A natural cataclysm may have all but obliterated their remains from the face of the earth, an event of such unimaginable magnitude that what had previously been a temperate zone was covered in a relatively short span of time by a seemingly eternal mantle of ice.

Do such notions as an abrupt polar shift or tsunamis which could destroy all traces of cities and cultures fly in the face of accepted scientific orthodoxy? And yet how else are we to explain the presence among us of so many phenomena which stubbornly resist fitting into the officially accepted reconstruction of our past?

The notion of a prehistoric civilization that lived and traveled around the islands and rim of the Pacific is one which has intrigued a number of scholars over the years. But there is another theory, one that reaches, or according to most established thinking even surpasses, the absolute boundaries of responsible scholarship. This is the theory of the lost continent of the Pacific, known either as Lemuria or Mu.

Nineteenth-century scientists hypothesized a large land mass that filled most of what is now the Indian Ocean in order to account for the presence of certain species of lemurs in areas widely separated by water, such as Madagascar and parts of Asia. A scientist named Philip L. Sclater coined the name

Lemuria for this hypothetical land mass, and the name has subsequently been used for a continent which is supposed by some to fill a substantial part of the Pacific Ocean.

The most dedicated advocate in this century of a vanished Pacific continent is Colonel James Churchward, who claimed to have discovered the secrets of this lost land through the deciphering of what he calls the Naacal Tablets, which he was introduced to during his service in India and also through legends of the Pacific and Indian America. He called the land mass Mu, a name given to the lost continent by the Hawaiians. In a series of books, beginning with *The Lost Continent of Mu*, Churchward states that Mu was, in fact, the cradle of all civilization and the home of the true Garden of Eden. He says that this first human civilization arose about 80,000 years ago, and that Mu had a population of up to 64,000,000. All subsequent cultures in his theory diffused from that starting point.

The world of Mu vanished completely due to a natural catastrophe of epic proportions, according to Churchward. Thirteen thousand years ago, enormous gas belts located in vast caverns deep beneath the surface of the earth collapsed, and the entire continent was destroyed, along with all but a very few of its inhabitants. These few survivors are the ones who ultimately bore the torch of learning and achievement to the rest of the world.

While such independent thinking is reminiscent of science fiction, it might be well to ascertain whether there is any scientific basis for the disappearance of a mid-Pacific continent.

A very reputable scholar named Thomas Gold, holder of the John L. Wetherill Chair in Astronomy at Cornell University and Director of the Center for Radiophysics and Space Research, has lately advanced what he calls the Deep-Earth-Gas

182

Hypothesis. His articles on the subject have appeared in a number of highly esteemed scientific journals.

Gold theorizes that the greater part of the earth's natural gas reserves are not, as had previously been assumed, the product of organic decomposition, but rather are to be found in pockets deep within the earth. He observes that oil and gas fields have a clear association with regions where earthquakes are most likely. These pockets of gas can be released by earthquakes, and under certain circumstances may even be the cause of seismic disturbance.

The gases are held in what Gold calls pore-space domains—porous rock formations which become unstable as they reach a certain depth. When that critical depth is reached, the bottom pores will collapse and those at the top will release their gas. This is likely to happen "along the crustal faults and fissures of the tectonic plate boundaries."

One cannot be quite so cavalier about Churchward's gas belts when such a theory begins to gain respectability in present-day scientific circles.

At the same time, it has been estimated that to build the city of Nan Madol in the Carolines, the huge statues of Easter Island, the temples at Tonga, the ancient buildings at Tinian, New Caledonia, Malden, Rarotonga, and at other selectively small islands in the Pacific, a land area thirty times the size of the present islands would be needed to support a population large enough to construct the abandoned stone walls, buildings, and cities.

Indeed, the prospect of being able to find definitive answers to the questions raised about these mysteries of Oceania seems rather remote. The real answers, if such there be, are likely to lie either on the floor of the Pacific, or buried deep in layers of shifting ocean-bottom silt.

Another answer is that of traditional memory—a memory shared by the inhabitants of many of the Pacific islands, of extensive lands long gone, of vanished empires, and of the building of great cities before the land sunk and the ocean rose as a result of a sudden cataclysm. One memory of former empires and tribute exacted was so tenacious that Yap islanders still carved enormous eight-foot-diameter stone tribute coins for delivery to islands long forgotten.

When the Pacific began to be explored and colonized in modern times, the difference between the civilization level of the island peoples whom the explorers encountered and their predecessors who had built cities and established empires was observed with great interest. Some of the islanders practiced cannibalism, considered by behavioral scientists to be a reversion to barbarism—a forced reversion occurring when there was no other protein available to satisfy their needs. In view of their former advanced development, knowledge, distance navigation, and massive architecture, the isolation and recession of the islanders might be better understood within the context of a sudden and cosmic catastrophe.

Explorers and traders from Asia made occasional forays into the Pacific islands but had not annexed any except those close to the Asian continent. China possessed great commercial and military seagoing junks during the Ming dynasty but interrupted her penetration of the South Sea (Nan Yang) about the time of the beginning of the Ching dynasty—China's last. Territorial penetration and annexation were eventually carried out by Japan—especially after World War I, when Japanese rule was established in a number of former German colonies, the Carolines, Marquesas, for example. Here Japanese control lasted until the latter part of World War II when they came under United States administration.

One of these islands, Eniwetok, was used in 1947 for a United States atom bomb land and sea experiment. The native population was resettled on other islands and then, in 1968, were given a chance to vote on whether they wanted to return to their homeland, where the United States government had spent years cleaning up the radioactivity. The islanders voted to return to their island and when they did so were pleased to find that new coconut trees had been planted for them. But before they could express their thanks they were told not to eat the coconuts as the new trees were still "hot" and presumably dangerous.

12

Atomic Warfare— Ancient and Modern

For several years after World War II, the United States limited its work on nuclear weapons to mostly lab studies and cerebral and ethical pursuits. The issue of whether or not we should have used the bomb was being heatedly debated all around the globe. Even some of the scientists who had invented the bomb looked upon their creation as a sort of Frankenstein monster. That which had been created to save the lives of millions of American troops from a direct invasion of Japan may have truly become the greatest life-threatening force humanity has ever known.

However, by the mid-1950s, scientific and military leaders began an active, above-ground program of nuclear testing. Eniwetok, an island atoll used as a base during the Pacific war, became ground zero for a test bomb. Another testing site was the Bikini atoll, whose end-of-the-world connotation became the inspiration for the name of a brief bathing suit.

Fashion considerations aside, the Bikini blast had a more significant, if less-discussed, repercussion. On March 1, 1954, the test blast went off. Crew members on a Japanese fishing vessel reported seeing a bright flash of whitish-yellow light in the west. It was followed by a mysterious fall of ashes which covered the deck of their ship. Though they were outside the U.S. government's restricted zone, the crew had been covered with radioactive dust. And as they continued their journey west, they became sluggish, and some suffered yellowish discharge from their eyes. Out of a crew of twenty-four all became critically ill—and one died—from radiation poisoning.

By the mid-1960s, the U.S. was not the only country with nuclear capabilities. The French were testing in the Pacific also, on an island called Mururoa. And the British were testing ten-kiloton bombs in the Australian outback. And, of course, the USSR had constructed a fission bomb. The results of these above-ground tests were striking—and frightening. After some testing, the skies above the Hawaiian Islands turned pink, green, and finally—blood-red.

World public opinion turned against the atmospheric testing of atomic devices, where radiation could contaminate the air or sea. Thus, as part of a 1962 test-ban treaty, both the United States and the Soviet Union agreed to limit their nuclear testing to underground blasts.

Initial underground testing in the United States was carried on in Nevada, but the blasts were felt as earthquake activity sufficient to shake buildings in Las Vegas and nearby areas.

The government had to find another site for its testing, one even more remote than the deserts of New Mexico and Nevada. The answer was found in the barren wilderness of

Alaska, on the island of Amchitka, a seventy-five-mile, barren splinter of rock in the Aleutian Islands chain. The U.S. had used the island during World War II as a mobilizing base against the Japanese invasion of Attu and Kiska. After the war, the government had given little thought to the area until they needed an uninhabited locale for underground blasts. Amchitka seemed to be a perfect choice, and a small test bomb, code-named Milrow, was detonated there in 1969.

When the Atomic Energy Commission (AEC) decided to use Amchitka for a more major test in 1971, it faced a sudden storm of protest from state residents and their representatives. Amchitka was situated in the Ring of Fire, the belt of earthquake zones which surrounds the Pacific. Alaskans had a special reason to be aware of this phenomenon, since their state had been struck by the largest-scale earthquake in recorded history just recently in 1964. A nuclear explosion in such a seismically unstable area could possibly set off new tremors and usher in an even more destructive catastrophe.

Although a White House report agreed that this could be a serious problem, their experts assured all that there was really no danger. The AEC engineers were certain they had prepared for all contingencies. After the Milrow test, when scientists examined the island, they found less than a five-inch shift in the ground. Plans went ahead for the test of the larger warhead. This was a five-megaton bomb called Cannikin.

The Cannikin device would explode only one mile below the earth's surface (a distance of 5,875 feet). The drill bit was ten feet wide, rather than the usual six-inch bit used to drill for oil. The bit removed over 450,000 pounds of earth and rock from the heart of Amchitka Island. And Cannikin was rated as the equivalent of at least ten billion pounds of TNT, over 250 times the energy dropped on Hiroshima. The resulting blast would leave the island's surface hotter than the surface of the sun.

When Canada and Japan heard of the proposed testing, they too issued formal protests. Their shores would be exposed to any tsunami raised should the test go wrong. Peru and Sweden raised their voices in complaint; thirty-five U.S. Senators petitioned the Nixon administration to cancel the test. It did not. The U.S. government, the AEC, and the Council of Environmental Quality all assured the public that they need not worry.

On November 6, 1971, the bomb exploded. And though no earthquakes or tidal waves occurred, what effect did that explosion have on the structure of that region?

Some might say that our scientists were right and we had nothing to fear. All facts and figures have been taken into account, and the amount of nuclear activity that we have caused is well within the earth's tolerance.

However, an earthquake at Tablas, Iran, in 1978 seems to call these comfortable calculations into question. Twenty-five thousand people died in a strangely shallow earthquake—a mere thirty-six hours after a Soviet underground atomic test in southern Siberia.

Then, too, today's scientists think only of humankind's nuclear activities in the past forty-four years. But even some of the bomb's creators had a belief that they were not the first humans to unleash the power of the atom.

Robert Oppenheimer, the father of the atomic bomb, was also knowledgeable in ancient Sanskrit writings. At the time of the Trinity test, he was heard to quote from the *Mahabharata*:

> *If the radiance of a thousand suns*
> *Were to burn at once in the sky,*
> *That would be like the splendor of the Mighty One . . .*
> *I am become Death—the destroyer of worlds.*

Still later, when engaged in a question and answer session with a group of students in 1952, Oppenheimer was asked if the Trinity bomb had been the first to be detonated. His answer is provocative: "Well—yes. In modern times, of course."

What if, as Oppenheimer apparently suspected, mankind had already gone through a nuclear age thousands of years before?

Some scientists and scholars have turned to the ancient writings of past civilizations such as the *Ramayana*, the Puranic Vedic texts, and other Sanskrit writings. One in particular, the *Mahabharata*, describes a weapon known as the *Agneya*:

> It was a single projectile
> Charged with all the power of the universe.
> An incandescent column of smoke and flame
> As bright as ten thousand Suns
> Rose in all its splendor . . .
> It was an unknown weapon,
> An iron thunderbolt,
> A gigantic messenger of death
> Which reduced to ashes
> The entire race of the Vrishnis and the Andhakras
> . . . The corpses were so burned
> As to be unrecognizable.
> Their hair and nails fell out;
> Pottery broke without apparent cause,
> And the birds turned white.

Another set of ancient writings, the Tibetan *Stanzas of Dzyan*, describes a war as follows:

> The chief of all the Yellow-faced was sad, seeing the evil intentions of the Dark-faced. He sent his air vehicles to all his brother chiefs . . .
> The Lords of the Dark-eyed have prepared their magic Agneyastra. . . . Come, and use yours.
> Let every Lord of the Dazzling Face ensnare the air

vehicle of every Lord of the Dark-faced, lest any of them escape.

. . . The kings reached then the safe lands in their air vehicles, and arrived in the lands of fire and metal. . . .

Stars showered on the lands of the Dark-faced while they slept. The speaking beasts remained quiet. The Lords waited for orders but they came not, for their masters slept.

If the Sanskrit fragment describes a nuclear weapon, could the Tibetan account be the description of a preemptive nuclear attack?

Many are the legends and writings around the world which speak of an ancient war—a war fought from sky-soaring vehicles, which rained a horrible new death upon their enemies, a war of great iron projectiles that flew through the skies and leveled homes, annihilating races.

And what of the ruins of Pakistan's Indus Valley? There geologists have found immense areas resembling major cities that are not mentioned in any of our known records. Forms of this culture may also be found at Easter Island in the Pacific region. The inhabitants of these cities are believed to be the ancestors of India's Dravidian race—a race of "Dark-faced" people.

Diggings reveal skeletons of people scattered around the area in postures similar to those at Pompeii, as if death came swiftly and with no hope of escape. Yet there is no sign of volcanic activity, and these skeletons contain a level of radioactivity comparable to that of Hiroshima and Nagasaki. Other findings indicate that both cities were destroyed about the same time in history.

Another such site can be found in southern Iraq, in the Euphrates valley. In 1947, archaeologists dug a mine shaft which passed through evidence of several ancient cultures. They encountered Babylonian, Chaldean, Sumerian, and many primitive cultural levels dating back some 8,000 years. At the lowest possible point they struck a level similar to fused glass. It wasn't noted until later that the only other similar surface structure could be found at Los Alamos—on the exact site of the Manhattan Project explosion.

Since then other sites around the world have been discovered and analyzed. Were these simply sites where some extreme natural phenomena had occurred, or has the earth already experienced a nuclear age—and a nuclear catastrophe?

If the earth has, what changes or horrors has this brought about? Did other civilizations, especially in the Pacific region, watch as a nuclear war wiped them from the planet? Did those explosions cause earthquakes that changed the very configuration of their regions?

Considering the destructive capabilities of a nuclear bomb, we can easily envision a world undergoing drastic changes. Whole land masses would have shifted, leveling mountains, sinking volcanic islands into the sea, and cracking the very heart of the earth's substructure. The aftermath would have left the remaining inhabitants a whole new world to adjust to and explore—and fear.

And what of the radiation's effect on the magnetic poles of our planet? or on animal life? What species would have been wiped from the face of the earth? And what new forms of life—in all its myriad possibilities—would have formed?

Studying the ancient writings from India, Asia, and even the Native American and Native Canadian cultures, we are forced to consider that so similar a tale of destruction, found in so many different cultures, is provocative indeed.

There are numerous reports of military and nuclear vessels sinking in the Dragon Triangle. Several Soviet submarines and at least one U.S. fighter carrying an atomic bomb are among those lost in the center of those mysterious waters. As many as 126 warheads may have disappeared beneath the waves.

Can there be a force below the sea stockpiling these nuclear weapons? And is it doing this as a form of protecting us from ourselves, or preparing for some counterstrike? Could there be some ancient mechanism, thousands of years old, preparing to ward off its hated foe?

It is instructive to note that the most famous disappearance of recent times, the vanishing of Flight 19, occurred halfway around the world in the Bermuda Triangle—and happened less than five months after the dropping of the atomic bomb. Had that blast awakened something deep in the waters of the Dragon Triangle? Something that could reach across the world and affect another area of anomalies?

Others might tie all of these tales and strange occurrences to the UFO phenomenon. It has been speculated that we are always under the observing eyes of some alien life form. Were they the forerunners of our civilization and did they bring about their own destruction? Or are we part of some terrible experiment of theirs? Will they watch as we create and loose our atomic might upon ourselves, again and again?

Some Oriental philosophers have also considered the significance of Yin and Yang, that all universal force moves in a circle. Could mankind be trapped in a never-ending cycle of watching his civilization rise and fall?

All these things are a consideration as we view the effect of nuclear power. And as we meditate upon the many forms of destruction and mutation that such power can bring about, we must look to the area of the Dragon Triangle, and wonder what lies beneath its surface. What has it done with all of the people? the vessels of war? And most important, what has happened to the deadly cargoes—the nuclear warheads these vessels carried?

13

Doorway to the Future . . . or the Past?

A great deal had happened to the earth and to humanity before our own accounts of early civilization began to be recorded about six thousand years ago. Our knowledge of history does not indicate a continued progress over the six-thousand-year period but rather a series of developments and retrogressions until, over the last several centuries, a technical civilization spread throughout the world. Although our present communications and technical advances are more highly developed than in any previous time in our known history, we still live in a period of uncertainty, menaced by natural catastrophes as well as those caused by our own still developing powers of destruction, technical potentialities which should be better employed for the protection of the planet and its inhabitants.

We can look at a time line of the 6,000-year triumphal march of our culture, hunting and herding, the great leap to agriculture, early cities, pyramids and ziggurats, Greece, Rome, the Middle Ages, up to our present pinnacle of culture. And the 100,000 years of prehistory?

Our view of that span of nonhistory, enough time to reproduce our march to culture sixteen times, is simple. Humanity spent it shivering in caves, being eaten by sabertoothed tigers and cave bears, and eating the occasional mammoth.

This rather simplistic world outlook has been challenged, not merely today, but in ancient times, as Plato relates in a supposed conversation between the great Athenian lawgiver, Solon, and an Egyptian hierophant who took the Greeks to task:

> In mind you are all young; there is no old opinion handed down among you by ancient tradition, nor any science that is hoary with age. And I will tell you the reason . . . there have been and will be again many destructions of mankind arising out of many causes . . . thus you have to begin all over again as children; and know nothing of what happened in ancient times among us or among yourselves. . . .
>
> In the first place, you remember one deluge only, whereas there were many of them. . . .

Mystery in our world is something removed from everyday existence, pushed to the very boundaries—far off into space, down into the subatomic realm. Mystery is not a part of our lives, and the words "we don't know" are almost inconceivable.

Thus we are unprepared for storms where wind and waves

can so batter a structure that a metal ladder is twisted like a pretzel. Could such storms be predicted more accurately? Couldn't they be stopped?

We are not prepared when the seemingly solid earth shrugs, sending the best creations of our cherished culture tumbling down in ruin. This does not accord with our worldview. And the survivors wonder, could this not have been predicted? Could it not have been prevented?

Many places around the earth right now are ticking bombs, yet millions of people live and work in zones where major earthquakes are expected—Tokyo, with thirty million people in its metropolitan area; Los Angeles, with ten million living on and near the San Andreas Fault.

We continue to build our technological marvels on ground that can give way. The 1964 Alaskan earthquake and its attendant tsunami destroyed half the homes in Valdez, wrecked or rendered uninhabitable every major commercial building, and totally demolished the town's waterfront. Where did we situate the southern terminus of the Alaskan Oil Pipeline? Valdez.

There may come a day when the recent Exxon oil spill will be considered a minor inconvenience compared to the oil catastrophe caused by an earthquake. And with its effect on our nation's oil supply, this catastrophe will be felt by everyone in this country. Can we pinpoint the coming tremor's strength and location? Will we know when it's coming?

We cannot comprehend the power of a seismic water wave that can strike a low-lying island, sweeping away houses, people, and even all the surface vegetation as easily as we sweep the dust from the top of a table. Our science may have reached the point now where we can warn against tsunamis, once they've been discovered (that is, after they've struck once). But on receiving the warning, our only option is to head for the high ground—and stay out of Nature's way.

In the face of such natural catastrophes, our vaunted science seems small indeed. And despite its theoretical explanations of the causes of these and other cataclysms, science has as little effect on the outcomes of such disasters as the priests and shamans who ascribed them to the actions of deities, demons—or dragons. Does it make the tragedy any more comprehensible to say that an airplane has been smashed by an eddy in an invisible air current moving 200 miles per hour through the sky than to say it had been struck from the sky by an angry god?

To encounter any of these natural phenomena would be sufficient to shake the underpinnings of belief in the logical, orderly world that orthodoxy would have us believe we live in. But what is one to make of a zone where all of these natural disasters are commonplace, and where anomalies beyond the natural laws are to be found as well? How does one explain a triangle on the earth's surface where the finest examples of our marine and aviation technology simply . . . disappear?

Before we dismiss the notion that such things do indeed occur in nature, let us look at the phenomenon of the black hole. Suspected, but never seen, black holes may be the gateway to universes beyond our own. Such sinkholes in the fabric of space were first postulated by the German astronomer Karl Schwarzschild in 1916. Schwarzschild suggested the existence of a mass so dense that nothing, not even light, would be able to escape its gravity.

Everything within the black hole's immediate vicinity is inexorably sucked toward its center, what physicists call a "singularity," the point of infinite density where the laws of space and time as we know them break down and fall apart. The point of no return for energy and objects being drawn toward the singularity is known as the "event horizon."

Although a black hole has never been directly detected, astronomers think it is formed when the matter in immense stars suddenly collapses on itself. Black holes may lie at the center of our own galaxy, at the heart of quasars (highly active, quasi-stellar energy sources) and even in some binary star systems.

Theoreticians like Cambridge mathematician Roger Penrose have formulated a potentially unique use for black holes. An astronaut, for example, might be able to plunge below the event horizon of a particularly massive, rotating black hole and emerge in another universe altogether, or reemerge in our own universe, vast distances away, at the same instant. A third alternative is that our adventurous astronaut could enter into a negative universe where nature is upside down. Gravity, for instance, might appear more like a repelling than an attracting force.

To accomplish such a feat requires the existence of the black hole's opposite, the "white hole," which spews matter and energy *out* of its singularity and beyond the event horizon.

Presently the search for both supermassive objects goes on, especially for possible black holes among the star clusters. One of the leading candidates in the search is the Star Cygnus X-1 in the constellation Cygnus. The search is of considerable import, since if our earth or solar system came too close to a large enough black hole, it could theoretically be sucked into it, totally modifying, compressing, or destroying all matter with which we are familiar and perhaps spewing it out again in a different form.

It seems incredible that the astronomy of our time, after only several hundred years of practice and research, has been able to identify the secrets—and dangers—present in the distant stars. But has our cosmic knowledge been so recent? Clay tablets kept by the Sumerians 5,000 years ago refer to a danger star, called by them the "demon bird of Nergal." Nergal was the powerful and sinister lord of the underworld. And the dangerous "demon bird," when translated and located on their star-charts, turns out to be *our* Cygnus X-1.

At our present stage of knowledge, we can only take the first step to wisdom in coming to grips with phenomena such as the magnetic anomalies of the Dragon Triangle—and admit our ignorance. Study is just beginning on the magnetic component of tectonic activity, about the magnetic anomalies sometimes detected near volcanoes, and about the strange weak and strong spots in the earth's own magnetic field. In spite of considering magnetism the servant of anyone with a pocket compass, we know next to nothing about the powers and potentialities of the electromagnetic energy generated by our planet.

Although we have used the surface of the oceans for centuries to carry our trading and naval vessels, it is only in the last three generations that we have had the technology to explore the deep. Up to that point, such explorations as could be attempted were accomplished by men without protective suits, and whose air supply was limited to the capacity of their lungs.

Today, we boast that we have charted the ocean depths. But the map is not the territory. We have actually visited only a tiny fraction of the nearly 130,000,000 square miles of the ocean floor. Do we really know all the denizens of these deeps?

Recent history has proven orthodox science wrong, with at least one supposedly extinct species residing in the deep waters. Who knows what other creatures may be discovered? We do know the response of the orthodox, however. No less a scientist than Alexander von Humboldt faced derision from his supposed peers when he reported receiving from a marine animal a shock as strong as that from a Leyden jar. Today, everyone accepts the existence of the electric eel.

And again, until we have thoroughly examined the ocean

floors, who knows what remains—or artifacts—may be found? The seas have always been the repositories of our past, and it may be that they are the vaults of prehistory as well. Perhaps the day may come when submarine archaeologists will explore the lost cities of Lemuria, trying to determine what cataclysm sent them into the deeps. Or perhaps we may trigger a similar cataclysm ourselves.

Could the Dragon Triangle harbor watchers beneath the waves? If not human, perhaps mechanical, left over from the last great era of civilization, which, if the ancient sources are to be believed, destroyed itself with fire from the skies? Has our warlike use of the atom awakened long-dormant, long-sunken defenses from a millennia-old war? A war which both sides lost, literally bombing themselves into the Stone Age?

Is there any proof that such a war took place? There are excavated areas in Iraq, in the Soviet Republics near Iran, in Pakistan, and in Western China where the ground bears an astonishing resemblance to the "fused green glass" floor left in New Mexico by the first atomic bomb in 1945. And the great mysterious cities of Harappa and Mohenjo-Daro in Pakistan show high radioactivity in the skeletons buried in the ruins.

Legends of several cultures vividly recall what we would call atomic conflicts between nations millennia ago, leaving the world in a state of ruin and an apparent return to primitivism, a culture to which many survivors in the Pacific islands may have reverted. Natives of these islands living near the tremendous stone ruins they attribute to miraculous builders still retain legends of vastly more extensive lands under the sea, the sinking of which was caused by conflicts between the gods.

Survivors of such a conflict gradually recovered, and civilization resumed its upward march only to return to our present dilemma, confronted as we are with the same danger of atomic warfare.

Accounts of "atomic" wars of ten millennia ago are included in the ancient Indian epics, the *Mahabharata* and the *Ramanyana* (translated from Sanskrit into English since 1850). These were generally considered by their translators and readers to be a normal hyperbole associated with the magical conflicts of the ancient gods. They were, of course, not credited or even understood until 1945, when scholars as well as scientists noted striking coincidences in the size, description, and effect of these projectiles and the real atomic bomb.

If we do not fear submerged atomic death from ages past, there is more than enough to worry about from the present. In the last twenty years, as many as 120 nuclear warheads have been lost to the deep as attack submarines have vanished. And one aerial warhead was lost as well. Some may have been recovered with the salvage efforts on some of the submarines. But there are many warheads still sprinkled on the sea bed— too many for comfort, considering the sea bed in question, a sea bed racked with earthquakes, pocked with volcanoes.

Normal peacetime procedures would mean that none of the warheads would have been primed. But who can tell the effect on fissionable material caught in the fury of a volcanic eruption? To use a phrase all too common with reference to the Dragon Triangle—we don't know.

We may console ourselves with the thought that volcanic eruptions are fairly rare occurrences. However, even as this book goes to press, word comes of the formation of a new undersea volcano off Itō, southwest of Tokyo. The location— the Dragon Triangle.

Two mounds began to form in an area that previously had been mapped as flat. Their appearance was accompanied by thousands of earth tremors, and followed by the eruption of a volcano on the island of Kyushu. The color of the seawater in the area began to change. The fishing fleet of the port of Itō was evacuated in fear of a tsunami. This was the first eruption in that area in recorded history; this was a whole new volcano.

We can only be glad that this new addition to the world's volcano rolls did not appear beside the hulk of a sunken Soviet submarine, with its warheads and reactors, or the lost American fighter bomber. The thought of adding the power of a nuclear blast to a quake area is indeed terrifying. The resulting tsunamis could well scour the entire Pacific and all its coastline. In this case, we can only hope that the missing bombs remain hidden and permanently lost in the deep waters of the Dragon Triangle.

Can the strange geophysical traits of the Triangle bend the usual laws of the universe to afford us a window on the infinite? Could this be a portal for travelers from the unknown, who are simply passing through on their way to unguessed destinations? Do a few unlucky—or lucky—terrestrials find themselves taking journeys far longer than they had intended?

The tantalizing connection remains—strange lights and strange craft are seen in this place—seamen and airmen disappear in that place—as if off the face of the earth. Have they gone to experimentation, annihilation, slavery, or a galactic zoo? Do they find their way to other worlds? Worlds of wonder far beyond the familiar alternately comfortable and dangerous world we know? What would seem to be oblivion to us may be the beginning of a great adventure to those who have stepped through the gateways to other worlds.

The solving of the problems of Earth, social, economic, geopolitical, is a step toward the exploration of our solar system and, after that, the Universe. We have atomic power and, as in the story told in the Arabian Nights, we cannot put the genie back in the bottle. We must learn to use it in a positive and beneficial way.

In a united and peaceful Earth we can harness this cosmic power to the works of peace and exploration. As a united planet we can undertake the search for other worlds and other civilizations existing on planets among and beyond the stars.

Bibliography

Ashby, Gene. *A Guide to Ponape, An Island Argosy*. Eugene, OR: Rainy Day Press, 1983.

Berlitz, Charles. *The Bermuda Triangle*. New York: Doubleday, 1974.

————. *Doomsday: 1999 A.D.* Garden City, NY: Doubleday, 1981.

————. *Mysteries of Forgotten Worlds*. New York: Doubleday, 1972.

————. *World of Strange Phenomena*. New York: Wynwood, 1988.

Brown, Hugh Auchincloss. *Cataclysms of the Earth*. New York: Twayne, 1967.

Chatelain, Maurice. *La Fin du Monde*. Brussels: André de Raché Editions, 1982.

Childress, David. *Lost Cities of Ancient Lemuria and the Pacific*. Stelle, IL: Adventures Unlimited, 1988.

Cooper, Gordon. *Dead Cities and Forgotten Tribes*. New York: Philosophical Library, 1952.

Dos Passos, John. *Easter Island*. New York: Doubleday, 1971.

Edwards, Frank. *Stranger than Science*. New York: Lyle Stuart, 1956.

———. *Strangest of All*. New York: Ace Star, 1962.

Flemming, Nicholas. *Cities in the Sea*. New York: New English Library, 1971.

Gaddis, Vincent. *Invisible Horizons*. New York: World Horizons, 1965.

Godwin, John. *Unsolved: The World of the Unknown*. Garden City, NY: Doubleday, 1976.

Gwynn, Richard. *Way of the Sea*. Devon, England: Green Books, 1987.

Hapgood, Charles. *Maps of the Ancient Sea Kings*. Philadelphia: Chilton, 1966.

Heyerdahl, Thor. *Aku-Aku*. New York: Rand-McNally, 1958.

Lissener, Ivar. *The Living Past*. New York: Putnam, 1957.

The *Mahabharata*.

Mariani, Fosco. *Meeting with Japan*. New York: Viking, 1959.

Pauwels, Louis, and Jacques Bergier. *The Morning of the Magicians*. New York: Avon, 1963.

The *Ramayana*.

Sanderson, Ivan. *Investigating the Unexplained*. Englewood Cliffs: Prentice-Hall, 1972.

———. *Invisible Residents*. New York: World Publishing, 1960.

Soule, Gardner. *Men Who Dared the Sea*. New York: Crowell, 1976.

———. *Surprising Facts About Our World and Beyond*. New York: Putnam, 1976.

Steiger, Brad. *Mysteries of Time and Space*. Englewood Cliffs: Prentice-Hall, 1974.

Wilson, Colin. *Enigmas and Mysteries*. Garden City, NY: Doubleday, 1976.

VESSEL AND FLAG	TONNAGE	LAST MESSAGE	CREW PRESUMED LOST
Kuroshio maru #1 Japan	1,525	19 Apr. 1949	23
Kuroshio maru #2 Japan	1,525	22 Apr. 1949	22
Chōfuku maru #5 Japan	66	8 June 1952	29
Kaiō maru #5 Japan	500	24 Sept. 1952	31
Shinsei maru Japan	62	6 June 1953	17
Kōchi maru #16 Japan	150	Dec. 1953	22
Kuroshio maru #3 Japan	1,525	29 Jan. 1954	18
Fuyō maru #2 Japan	227	25 Sept. 1954	25
Seisho maru #1 Japan	190	20 Oct. 1954	25
Chiyo maru #15 Japan	18	6 Dec. 1954	12
F-3B Aircraft USA	—	26 June 1955	Not known
USAF *KB-50* Aircraft USA	—	12 Mar. 1957	8
USN *JD-1* Invader USA	—	16 Mar. 1957	5
USAF *C-97* Aircraft USA	—	22 Mar. 1957	67
Donan maru Japan	2,849	7 June 1963	33
Juno Panama	1,385	10 Oct. 1964	21
Denny Rose U.K.	6,656	13 Sept. 1967	42
Tong Hong U.K.	4,690	25 Oct. 1967	38
JA 341 Aircraft Japan	—	10 Feb. 1970	3
Junior KL Philippines	2,470	5 Oct. 1971	Not specified
P-2V Antisubmarine Patrol Aircraft Japan	—	16 July 1971	11
Sea Pine Panama	1,794	6 Oct. 1971	26
Geranium France	232	24 Nov. 1974	29
Transocean Shipper Philippines	9,275	16 Feb. 1975	33

VESSEL AND FLAG	TONNAGE	LAST MESSAGE	CREW PRESUMED LOST
Ming Song Panama	891	22 Oct. 1975	17
Berge Istra Liberia	227,912	29 Dec. 1975	40
Don Aurelio Panama	4,066	9 Jan. 1976	31
New Venture Panama	7,194	30 June 1976	30
Rose S Liberia	1,720	13 Feb. 1977	31
Hae Dang Wha South Korea	102,805	28 July 1980	29
Derbyshire U.K.	169,044	Sept. 1980	44
Dunav Yugoslavia	14,712	28 Dec. 1980	31
Antiparos Greece	13,862	2 Jan. 1981	35
Glomar Java Sea U.K.	5,930	Oct. 1983	81
Queen Jane Panama	9,909	23 Oct. 1987	24

SUBMARINES

DATE	CLASS	TYPE	LOCATION	CASUALTIES
Apr. 1968	Golf	Diesel/electric powered	Northwest of Japan	86 dead
1970	Alfa	Nuclear powered	Sea of Japan	Exact numbers of dead and survivors unknown
1971	Yankee	Nuclear powered	Near Guam	Crew numbers unknown — no survivors
Sept. 1974	Golf II	Diesel/electric powered	Southwest of Japan	No survivors
Nov. 1976	Foxtrot	Diesel/electric powered	Sea of Japan	Unknown
1977	Unidentified	Nuclear powered	South China Sea	Exact numbers unknown
Aug. 1980	Echo I	Nuclear powered	Sea of Japan	Exact numbers unknown
Oct. 1981	Whiskey	Diesel/electric powered	Northwest of Japan	Unknown
Sept. 1983	Charlie	Nuclear powered	Sea of Japan	90 dead
Mar. 1984	Victor I	Nuclear powered	West of Japan	Unknown
Sept. 1984	Echo II	Nuclear powered	60 miles west of Japan	Unknown
Sept. 1984	Golf II	Diesel/electric powered	Northwest of Oki Island	Unknown
Jan. 1986	Echo II	Nuclear powered	Sea of Japan	Unknown